Fresh
TOEIC

이정복 저

박영사

Preface

이 책은 저자가 30여 년 동안 대학에서 영어를 가르쳐 오면서 영어에 대한 정수만을 뽑아서 이해하기 쉽게 정리해 놓은 책이다. 이 책을 통해서 기초가 부족한 학생들은 영어에 대한 기초를 확립할 수 있을 것이고, 더 높은 수준의 학생들에게는 지금까지 공부해온 영어에 대한 보다 명확한 이해를 통해서 토익 실전문제의 풀이에도 어려움이 없을 것임을 확신한다. 이 책을 통해서 보다 더 넓은 영어의 바다에서 마음껏 헤엄치길 바란다.

이 책은 각 문법 분야에 대한 명확한 개념 정리와 풍부한 예문을 통해서 기초를 다지면서 바로 실전문제를 풀어볼 수 있도록 하였다. 진도를 나가면서 자연스럽게 영어의 진수를 맛볼 수 있다. 이를 통해서 대학생 여러분들에게 꼭 필요한 토익 점수 향상의 고지를 정복하고 각종 취업 시험 준비에도 그 책무를 다할 것임을 자부한다.

그리고 Self Review를 통해서 여러분들이 지금까지 배운 영어에 대해서 스스로 정리하고 확인해 볼 수 있도록 하였다. 이를 통해서 영어에 대한 여러분들의 위치를 가늠해 볼 수 있다는 데 의미가 크다.

물론, 영어는 하루아침에 완성되는 것은 아니다. 저자도 영어를 하루라도 보지 않으면 두려운 마음이 드는 것도 사실이다. 영어에 대한 꾸준한 관심과 반복 학습을 통해서 영어를 정복할 수 있다고 확신한다.

이 한 권의 책이 여러분들의 영어 정복을 위해 그 밑거름이 될 것임을 확신하면서 항상 여러분들의 앞날을 응원하며 건투를 빈다.

2021년 봄을 기다리며
저자 이 정 복

Contents

1 chapter

VERB

Chapter 1 VERB

▌문장 5형식의 기본구조

1. 주어(S) + 동사(V)
2. 주어(S) + 동사(V) + 보어(C)
3. 주어(S) + 동사(V) + 목적어(O)
4. 주어(S) + 동사(V) + 간접목적어(IO) + 직접목적어(DO)
5. 주어(S) + 동사(V) + 목적어(O) + 보어(C)

➡ 목적어의 유무에 따라 자동사, 타동사로 구별하고
  보어의 유무에 따라 완전, 불완전 동사로 나눈다.

Unit 01 주어(S) + 동사(V)

1. 기본 문형(S+V)

① I go home.
② The bird flies to the sky.

2. 주요 완전자동사

go, run, fly, rise, come, decline, happen, occur

rain, snow, exist, live, stand, stay

CheckUp 1. Select the best answer to complete each sentence.

1. As the human population (rises, raises), the animal and plant populations decrease.
2. He needs to (rise, raise) his grades in order to enter a good university.
3. Emma always (sits, seats) on the table.
4. Korea (lies, lays) between China and Japan.

---

3. 변형구문

There is(are)+명사

There remain+명사

There exist+명사

(단/복수의 일치는 동사 다음 단어, 즉 주어에 일치시켜야 함)

CheckUp 2. Select the best answer to complete each sentence.

1. There (is, are) a book on the desk.
2. There (remain, remains) many things for me to do.

Unit 02 주어(S) + 동사(V) + 보어(C)

1. 기본 문형(S+V+C)

① I am happy because I am rich.
② The man on the table is my English teacher.

2. 주요 불완전 자동사

be, become, remain(= stay)
seem/appear, prove/turn out,
look, smell, taste, sound, feel

CheckUp 3. Select the best answer to complete each sentence.

1. Mr. Kim is not a single. He (is, gets) married.
2. He stayed (calm, calmly).
3. It proved (false, falsely).
4. Two people walking on the beach look (sad, sadly).
5. The sweater feels (soft, softly).

3. 보어인 형용사 자리에 전명구

of importance 중요한, of use 쓸모 있는, out of stock 재고가 바닥난

Unit 03 주어(S) + 동사(V) + 목적어(O)

1. 기본 문형(S+V+O)

① I love BTS.
② He hates her.
③ I want to visit Brisbane.
④ She enjoys going to the movies.

⑤ I think that he is honest.

2. 순수 타동사: axx로 시작되는 건 모두 타동사

access, accompany, approach, approve, attend, arrange
(예외: arrive at/in, account for, apply for/to)

3. 앞뒤 전치사적 접두/접미어 붙은 건 모두 타동사

indicate, inspect, implement, enhance
contradict, overcome, join, anticipate
resemble, require, regret, reach
exceed, expand, express, expect
(예외: refer to, reply to, respond to, react to)

4. "말하다"라는 종류는 모두 타동사

mention, say, discuss, disclose, tell
(예외: talk, speak)

5. 기타 주의할 타동사

check
check the car/ the body/ the house. . .
check for the leak, check for the possible solution
face, present, provide
동사+사람+with 사물, 동사+사물+to 사람

6. 자동사가 3형식으로 쓸 때

with: deal with, agree with(on/to)
        interfere with, sympathize with, proceed with,
to: object to, return to,
at: laugh at, arrive at, look at(cf. look for, after, over, into)
for: look for, account for,

7. 동사와 명사가 같이 쓰이는 경우

access to, answer to, damage to, visit to
discussion about, question about, disclosure about,
regret for, influence on, interview with

Unit 04 주어(S) + 동사(V) + 간접목적어(IO) + 직접목적어(DO)

1. 기본 문형(S+V+IO+DO)

① He gave me a book.

② She bought me a new cell phone.

③ I asked her a question.

2. 주요 4형식 동사

give, offer, send, bring

ask, buy, cost, lend, show, tell

inform, notify, assure, remind

CheckUp 4. Select the best answer to complete each sentence.

1. The company sent (the bill me, me the bill).

2. He bought several new books (to his children, for his children).

3. I need the pen. Could you give (me it, it to me)?

---

3. 3형식으로 바꿀 때 즉 S+V+O+전명구로 바꿀 때 쓰이는 전치사 to, for, of

to: give, offer, send, bring, tell, show, teach

for: make, buy, get, cook, find

of: ask

① He gave some advice **to** me.

② She bought a new cell phone **for** me.

③ I asked a question **of** her.

4. 3형식 동사인데 4형식 동사로 오인할 수 있는 단어들

mention, explain, suggest, recommend, announce, introduce, prove, propose, describe, confess

(모두 4형식처럼 해석은 되지만, 3형식임. 따라서 "-에게 말하다"라고 할 때,

tell을 제외한 모든 "말하다"는 뜻을 가진 동사는 사람 앞에 "to"를 사용하여야 함)

Unit 05 주어(S) + 동사(V) + 목적어(O) + 목적보어(C)

1. 기본 문형(S+V+O+C)

① The song made BTS a big star.

② I want her to finish the work by Sunday.

③ He let me go there.

④ We regard it as uneconomical.

⑤ I call him Erick.

2. 형/~ing/p.p를 목적보어로 취하는 동사: make, keep, find

① I made her angry.

② This coat keeps her warm.

③ He found his mailbox empty.

3. to부정사를 목적보어로(동사들이 모두 미래지향적인 뜻)

설득류: persuade, convince, encourage, motivate, compel, force, tell, teach

허락류: permit, allow, enable,

바람류: expect, want, would like, require

권함류: cause, remind, invite, advise, ask,

☞ 특히, 수동태로 바뀌어도 to동사원형임을 숙지할 것

4. 원형동사를 목적보어로 취하는 동사

사역동사 +목적어 +원형, p.p (let, make, have)

get +목적어 +to원형, p.p (준사역동사)

지각동사 +목적어 +원형, -ing, p.p (see, hear, feel)

* **help** (to) 원형, **help** 목적어 (to) 원형

5. as+명사를 목적보어로(숙어로 외울 것)

"A를 B라 간주하다"

regard A as B, look on(upon) A as B, consider A as B, take A as B,

speak of A as B, refer to A as B, cite A as B, think of A as B,

define A as B, designate A as B

6. 명사를 목적보어로(be p.p +명사)

call, elect(be elected as B), consider A (as) B = A be considered B

appoint A (as) B = A is appointed (as) B

Practice Test A

✔ 다음 빈칸에 가장 적절한 것을 고르시오.

1) The sweater _____.
(A) feel soft   (B) feels soft   (C) feel softly   (D) feels softly

2) Who _____ that Korea will be united in the near future?
(A) think   (B) thinks   (C) is thinking   (D) are thinking

3) We _____ each other for more than ten years.
(A) know   (B) are knowing   (C) have known   (D) have been knowing

4) Your shoes are dirty. Could you _____?
(A) take off the shoes   (B) take off them
(C) take off it   (D) take them off

5) The climate _____ warmer every year.
(A) is   (B) gets   (C) is being   (D) is getting

6) After the interview I had to _____ a test.
(A) have   (B) take   (C) make   (D) give

7) A female penguin _____ one or two eggs each year.
(A) lay   (B) lays   (C) lie   (D) lies

8) Ms. Butler _____ as an architect in the Urban planning Institute..
(A) works   (B) working   (C) to work   (D) being worked

9) Henry gave _____.
(A) some flowers her   (B) some flowers to her
(C) some flowers for her   (D) to her some flowers

10) Because my mother cooks _____, her food tastes really _____.
(A) good – good   (B) good – well
(C) well – good   (D) well – well

Practice Test B

1) According to one definition, "avoidance" _____ behavior induced by adverse
   stimuli.
   (A) when   (B) in   (C) that   (D) is

2) Cedars _____ a particular variety of aromatic wood that repels insects.
   (A) having yields (B) yielding   (C) yields   (D) yield

3) He _____ a pioneer in American textile design and interior decoration.
   (A) who   (B) as   (C) was   (D) often

4) Hawthorne and Poe _____ in development of American short story.
   (A) who were leaders   (B) they were leaders
   (C) were both leaders   (D) who as leaders

5) Refrigerating meats _____ the spread of bacteria.
   (A) retards   (B) retarding   (C) to retard   (D) is retarded

6) Work _____ to generate electricity.
   (A) to be done   (B) it is done   (C) done by it   (D) must be done

7) The great Chicago fire in October, 1871, _____ much of the city and left
   about 100,000 people homeless.
   (A) that it destroyed   (B) that destroyed
   (C) was destroyed   (D) destroyed

8) "What's your opinion?" "It is imperative that they _____ there on time."
   (A) should   (B) shall   (C) be   (D) can be

9) Muscles _____ bones by pulling on tendons.
   (A) of moving   (B) move   (C) moving   (D) to move

10) Social reformer Jane Adams _____ a prominent role in the formation of
    the National Progressive party in 1912.
    (A) playing   (B) who played   (C) played   (D) to play

Practice Test C

☑️ 밑줄 친 부분 중 어법상 어색한 곳을 고르시오.

1) My book <u>was having</u> three <u>torn</u> pages, which I tried <u>to tape</u> before I <u>left</u>
             A   B   C   D

    home.

2) We like <u>to go</u> to the country <u>in spring</u> because the wild <u>flowers</u> smell so
            A   B   C

    <u>sweetly</u>.
       D

3) Insecticide is a chemical substance <u>that</u> is used to <u>die</u> insects, but you <u>must</u>
                                      A   B   C

    <u>not</u> overuse <u>it</u>.
             D

4) Here is <u>an</u> application form. Fill <u>out it</u> and then <u>give it back</u> to me when
            A   B   C

    you <u>are finished</u>.
            D

5) Ted and I <u>have</u> common <u>interests</u> and <u>similar</u> characteristics, so I always
              A   B   C

    <u>get him along with</u> well.
            D

6) Michael Scott is <u>the</u> director <u>who</u> <u>does</u> the important <u>decisions</u>.
                    A   B   C   D

7) I intend <u>to have</u> full advantage <u>of this trip</u> <u>to buy</u> <u>the things</u> we need.
          A   B   C   D

8) <u>Clouds</u> are formed <u>by a process</u> that <u>begins</u> when warm moist air <u>raises</u>.
  A   B   C   D

9) <u>Because of</u> the greenhouse effect, <u>the weather</u> of the Earth <u>is being</u>
    A   B   C

    <u>warmer</u> and warmer.
      C

10) <u>An</u> accident can <u>be happened</u> <u>at</u> any time and <u>any</u> where.
    A   B   C   D

Reading Comprehension

Questions 1–4 refer to the following letter.

Terry Adams
535 West Street,
Los Angeles, CA 94122

To Whom It May Concern;
I am pleased to receive your 1._____ of September 1, 2006 concerning the supply of our best computers. We are enclosing our price 2._____ and terms of business. We note that you have requested an additional discount of 5%, and we would like to point out that prices have already been cut to a 3._____. None of our 4._____ offer such discounts. We therefore regret that we are unable to allow you any further discount at the moment. In spite of the increased costs of raw materials expected next year, we anticipate being able to maintain present prices. We look forward to hearing from you.

Your truly,

Edwin Fetcher

1. (A) explanation   (B) information
   (C) expression   (D) inquiry

2. (A) model   (B) selection
   (C) list   (D) listing

3. (A) minimum   (B) minimal
   (C) marginal   (D) margin

4. (A) compete   (B) competitors
   (C) competition   (D) competitive

Questions 5-7 refer to the following announcement.

Good afternoon everyone. I'm afraid we're going to be very busy this afternoon, but before we get started, I would just like to make a short announcement about the new sick leave policy. As of the first of the month, if any employee is absent for 3 days or more, you must provide a doctor's note on your return to work. If you are sick for less than three days, you don't need a doctor's note but your manager or supervisor must be informed as soon as possible. There is a maximum of 9 sick days per employee per year except in exceptional circumstances.

5. What is the purpose of this announcement?
   (A) To note changed sick leave policy
   (B) To let employees know a new timetable
   (C) To announce a doctor's office to be open
   (D) To give a warning to new employees

6. When do employees need a doctor's note?
   (A) When they are absent for 1 day
   (B) When they are absent for 2 days
   (C) When they are absent for 4 days
   (D) It is not necessary to provide a doctor's note.

7. When do employees NOT need a doctor's note?
   (A) When they are absent for 3 days
   (B) When they are absent for 3 days or more
   (C) When they are absent for less than 3 days
   (D) When they are absent for 7 days

Self Review

☑ 동사에 대해 아는 대로 써보세요. 그리고 다시 한번 복습하시기 바랍니다!!!

S+V	
S+V+C	
S+V+O	
S+V+I.O+D.O	
S+V+O+V+O.C	

2 chapter

TENSE

Chapter 2 TENSE

시제는 크게 기본시제, 완료시제, 진행시제로 대별된다. 중요하게 취급되는 시제는 현재시제, 현재완료시제, 시간, 조건 부사절에서 미래를 대신하는 현재시제로 볼 수 있다.

구분	과거	현재	미래
기본 3시제	-ed, 불규칙동사 과거형	원형동사, 원형(e)s	will/shall+동사원형
기본 3진행형	was/were +ing	am/are/is +ing	will/shall+be+ing
완료형	had+p.p	have/has+p.p	will/shall+have+p.p
완료 진행형	had been +ing	have/has+been-ing	will/shall+have been-ing

Unit 01 현재시제와 미래시제

1. 기본 용법

현재시제는 현재를 중심으로 지속성, 반복성, 계속되는 습관이나 상태를 나타낸다.

① He usually studies English.

② Every Sunday she goes to church.

③ The earth goes around the Sun.

④ I live in Daegu.

CheckUp 1. Select the best answer to complete each sentence.

1. Water (boils, is boiling) at 100 degree Celsius.

2. The water (boils, is boiling). Could you turn off the stove?

3. In Korea it (snows, is snowing) a lot in winter.

4. Every year, the company (provides, is providing) a variety of products and services for customers.

5. A good manager always (encourages, is encouraging) the staff to do their best.

2. 미래시제 대신 현재시제를 사용하는 경우

① If it rains, I will stay home.

② The flight leaves(will leave) Daegu at 12:00.

CheckUp 2. Select the best answer to complete each sentence.

1. I don't know if it (rains, will rain) tomorrow.

2. The time will come when you (will understand, understand).

3. When I (see, will see) him, I will give him your message.

4. If it (will be, is) nice tomorrow, we'll go on a picnic.

5. I don't know if she (will come, comes) back soon.

---

3. 미래시제

① Next year I will be 20 years old.

② I am going to stop by your office tomorrow.

③ The meeting is to start in 20 minutes.

④ I am starting a new job.

CheckUp 3. Select the best answer to complete each sentence.

1. Many people (live, will live) to the age of 100 or more in the near future.

2. Mark and Vicky (are going to, will) get married next month.

3. "The phone is ringing." "I (am going to, will) answer it."

4. The investment company (has hired, will hire) two more analysts next week.

5. All the employees (get, will get) a regular medical checkup soon.

Unit 02 과거시제와 현재완료

1. 과거시제

① I met her three years ago.

② Hemingway wrote *The Old man and the Sea* in 1952.

③ He went to the movies last night.

Select the best answer to complete each sentence.

1. They (visited, have visited) China in 1996 for the first time.

2. My father doesn't live in Tokyo. He (lived, has lived) there when he was young.

3. Last night, all the employees in the factory (work, worked) overtime to meet the deadline.

4. Three days ago, Fiona (will say, said) at a news conference that she would quit her job next month.

2. 현재완료

① (계속) We have known each other since we were young.

② (경험) Have you ever been to Australia?

③ (완료) They have just arrived in Seoul.

④ (결과) He has gone to China.

3. 현재완료 주요문형

① 현재완료 + since + 주어 +과거형 동사

② 현재완료 + for + 숫자(for대신, in/over도 가능)

* 현재완료와 자주 쓰이는 부사 already/ just, ever/never/yet 등

① I have been in Canada since 1997.

② We have studied English for three years.

③ She has played the piano since she was a child.

④ Jane left New York in 1995 and she has lived in Seoul since then.

CheckUp 5. Select the best answer to complete each sentence.

1. Mr. Hall (commutes, has commuted) to work by subway for three years.

2. I (am waiting, have been waiting) for Jane for two hours.

3. By the time Professor Scott retires next year, he (has been teaching, will have been teaching) for 30 years.

4. Jack (visited, has visited) Seoul three times since 1998.

5. Matthew (lived, has lived) in Seoul since he was young.

Unit 03 과거완료와 미래완료

1. 과거완료시제

반드시 과거시제와 함께 쓰여야 함

① (계속) I had studied English for 10 years before I took the test.

② (경험) I had never seen the movie until then.

③ (완료) By the time I got there, I had already traveled 100 kilometers.

④ (결과) I had lost some weight but looked healthier.

2. 대과거

대과거는 과거에 일어난 일보다 어떤 일이 먼저 일어난 일을 표시하기 위해 사용

① I lost the book that I had bought the day before.

② No sooner had she heard the news than she began to cry.

    = Hardly had she heard the news before she began to cry.

CheckUp 6. Select the best answer to complete each sentence.

1. The patient (enters, had entered) the consulting room before the doctor was ready.

2. When Mark accepted the job, it (had been, was) vacant for the past year.

3. I learned that the Korean War (broke, had broken) out in 1950.

---

3. 미래완료

미래를 기준으로 현재의 일이나 상태가 완료되거나 계속되거나 경험되어지는 것

① (완료) I will have completed the work by two o'clock.

② (경험) I will have read this book three times if I read it again.

③ (계속) She will have been ill for three years by tomorrow.

CheckUp 7. Select the best answer to complete each sentence.

1. When Mr. Kim retires next month, he (will teach, will have taught) for twenty years.

2. Bill (will finish, will have finished) his novel by the time he comes back from his trip to Venice.

---

4. by + 미래표시: 미래완료나 미래를 정답으로 할 것

   by + 과거표시: 과거완료를 정답으로 할 것

5. recently는 현재완료나 과거시제와 주로 쓰임

CheckUp 8. Select the best answer to complete each sentence.
1. Recently, the publishing company (moves, has moved) to a larger office space.
2. We (receive, received) a letter from him recently.

---

6. 주장, 명령, 요구, 제안, 충고를 나타내는 동사, 형용사, 명사가 있으면 원형동사가 정답

   (예, insist, suggest, demand, order, recommend, request, 등)
   * 이성 판단의 형용사도 마찬가지(essential, necessary, important 등)

   ① He insisted that she change her clothes.
   ② We suggested that he be rewarded for his hard work.
   ③ It is necessary that we learn from our experience.
   ④ It is important that you solve the problem yourself.

   cf. He insisted that she changed her clothes.
      Her expression suggested that she was angry.

Unit 04 진행형

1. 현재진행, 과거진행, 미래진행

종류	예문
현재진행 am/are/is -ing	It is raining outside now. I am studying English now. They are having a good time with friends. He is always complaining.
과거진행 was/were -ing	I was playing soccer when you called last night. You were studying English when I called you.
미래진행 will be -ing	I will be studying when you come home.

CheckUp 9. Select the best answer to complete each sentence.

1. When you called me last night, I (am watching, was watching) the news on TV.

2. Beethoven (lost gradually, was gradually losing) his hearing in his twenties.

2. 완료진행

종류	예문
현재완료진행 have/has been –ing	She **has been playing** the piano since this morning. I **have been working** since two o'clock.
과거완료진행 had been –ing	I **had been waiting** for an hour when you came. It **had been raining** for ten days when the river flooded.
미래완료진행 will/shall have been –ing	I **will have been learning** English for 10 years.

3. 진행형, 수동태 불가 동사들

구분	종류
소유	belong, have, own, possess
상태	include, resemble, consist of, appear, exist
인식	know, see, hear, think, taste
감정	love, like, hate, wish, want

CheckUp 10. Select the best answer to complete each sentence.

1. The president (likes, is liking) to play golf on weekends.

2. The mystery still (is remaining, remains) unsolved.

Practice Test A

☑️ 다음 빈칸에 가장 적절한 것을 고르시오.

1) The meeting always _____ on time.
(A) starts   (B) is starting   (C) has started   (D) has been starting

2) My brother and I _____ smoke, but we don't anymore.
(A) use   (B) use to   (C) used to   (D) are used to

3) In most countries, doctors must pass an examination to be licensed when
   they _____ medical universities.
(A) finish   (B) finishes   (C) will finish   (D) will have finished

4) I _____ you last night, but I forgot.
(A) am going to call   (B) was going to call
(C) will call   (D) would call

5) Irene left New Hampshire in 1986 and _____ in Tokyo since then.
(A) worked   (B) has worked   (C) will work   (D) would work

6) The population of the world _____ rapidly.
(A) grow   (B) grows   (C) is growing   (D) are growing

7) The class _____ to room 101.
(A) has changed   (B) been changed
(C) has been changed   (D) had changed

8) _____ practicing with the band this week?
(A) Paul been   (B) Has Paul
(C) Has been Paul   (D) Has Paul been

9) I realized that we _____ before.
(A) meet   (B) met   (C) have met   (D) had met

10) By the middle of the twenty-first century, the computer _____ a
    necessity in every home.
(A) become   (B) has become   (C) had become   (D) will have become

Practice Test B

1) The staff meeting _____ on the first Monday of every month.
(A) holds   (B) is held   (C) held   (D) has held

2) Yesterday, we _____ a meeting to discuss the recent security incidents in Georgetown.
(A) attend   (B) attended   (C) had attended   (D) will attend

3) The company _____ two new factories and hire at least 600 more workers over the next few months.
(A) will open   (B) opened
(C) had been opening   (D) has opened

4) The economic outlook was discouraging until the beginning of this year, but things _____ since then.
(A) improve   (B) improved   (C) will improve   (D) have improved

5) When Mr. Han returned from his business trip, he realized that his office _____ into.
(A) had been broken   (B) broke
(C) would be broken   (D) broken

6) Susan _____ all three projects by the end of August next year.
(A) completes   (B) has completed
(C) completed   (D) will have completed

7) When she came into the office, the manager _____ on the phone.
(A) talks   (B) talked   (C) will talk   (D) was talking

8) The airline _____ from financial problems since the Asian crisis began.
(A) suffered   (B) is suffered
(C) has been suffering   (D) will suffer

9) My father currently _____ a fancy car made in Germany.
(A) own   (B) owns   (C) is owning   (D) owned

10) Mr. Frank will arrive at the convention center right before the meeting of shareholders _____.
(A) begins   (B) will begin   (C) had begun   (D) began

Practice Test C

✅ 밑줄 친 부분 중 어법상 어색한 것을 고르시오.

1) There <u>is</u> a report in <u>today's</u> newspaper that <u>there is</u> a big traffic accident
        A   B   C
  near Incheon late <u>last</u> night.
                      D

2) Summer vacation <u>begins</u> <u>next</u> week, and I <u>go</u> to Seattle <u>to visit</u> my
                      A   B   C   D
  grandparents.

3) <u>In</u> October 1957, Sputnik, the first <u>man-made</u> satellite, <u>had been launched</u>
  A   B   C
  <u>by</u> the Soviet Union.
  D

4) If you <u>call</u> her <u>at six</u> tomorrow, she probably <u>is practicing</u> <u>the</u> piano.
           A   B   C   D

5) <u>The</u> First World War <u>had begun</u> <u>in</u> 1914 and <u>ended</u> in 1918.
  A   B   C   D

6) Henry, <u>who</u> is now <u>in college</u>, <u>studies</u> English <u>for</u> ten years.
          A   B   C   D

7) We <u>have been having</u> an old Rolls Royce <u>that</u> we <u>bought</u> twenty years <u>ago</u>.
             A   B   C   D

8) <u>Since the arrival</u> of rock'n' roll <u>in the 1950s</u>, the music business <u>grows</u>
        A   B   C
  from a money maker to <u>a multimillion dollar monster</u>.
                                  D

9) <u>Don't</u> count your <u>chicken</u> before <u>they</u> <u>will be hatched</u>.
  A   B   C   D

10) A short time before <u>he</u> <u>died</u>, the old man <u>has written</u> <u>a will</u>.
                        A B   C   D

Reading Comprehension

Questions 1-4 refer to the following news article.

People who travel from country notice great differences in what 1._____ in various places can and cannot do. People in the United States have always enjoyed great personal freedom. They do not have to get 2._____ from the government to move from one city to another, from one house to another, or to change jobs. They are not required to carry 3._____ cards, and their right to life. liberty, and the 4._____ of happiness is guaranteed by the Constitution.

1. (A) individuals   (B) individuality
    (C) individually   (D) individualism

2. (A) remission   (B) competition
    (C) repetition   (D) permission

3. (A) identical   (B) identify
    (C) identification   (D) identity

4. (A) search   (B) pursuit
    (C) chase   (D) seeking

This Thursday, from 1 p.m. we will we conducting training related to the new computer system which has just been installed. Mrs. Crebbin will be running the training. It will take place from 1 p.m. to 6 p.m. in the main conference room. I would like to ask everyone to make every effort to be there on time and please read the relevant material which I put on your desks yesterday.

5. Which of the following are the employees NOT asked to do?
   (A) To attend the training
   (B) To be on time
   (C) To read the training material
   (D) To install the computer system

6. What will the training be about?
   (A) The computer system
   (B) The main conference room
   (C) New procedures
   (D) The software installation

7. Why is this announcement being made?
   (A) To announce that people can't use the computer system
   (B) To inform people of computer training
   (C) To tell people about installing a new computer system
   (D) To urge people to read the material

Self Review

☑ 시제에 대해 아는 대로 써보세요. 그리고 다시 한번 복습하시기 바랍니다!!!

현재시제	
미래시제	
과거시제	
현재완료	
과거완료	
미래완료	
현재진행형	
과거진행형	
미래진행형	
완료진행	

3
chapter

NOUN

명사는 셀 수 있는 가산명사와 셀 수 없는 불가산명사로 나누어 볼 수 있는데, 대부분이 가산명사이다. 얼마 되지 않는 불가산명사를 우선 숙지하고 나머지는 가산명사라고 생각하면 된다. 불가산명사는 부정관사나 복수형을 취하면 안된다. 가산명사는 관사를 붙이든 복수형태를 취해야 한다.

Unit 01 명사의 구조 및 종류

1. 역할로 구분: 주어, 목적어(타동사나, 전치사의 뒤), 보어자리

① He is a college student.

② He felt **the father** rise in him at the sight.

③ You can see the woman in **the little girl**.

④ A dog is **a faithful animal**.

CheckUp 1. Select the best answer to complete each sentence.

1. The study found (contaminating, contamination) in the river water.

2. (Joblessness, Jobless) has risen 2.5 percent since last year.

---

2. 수식/한정 받는 경우

```
관사
소유격
형용사
전치사        + 명사 +    전명구
타동사                   관계사절
명사 뒤(복합명사)         준동사(-ing, p.p, to부정사)
```

3. 명사의 종류: 보통, 집합, 물질, 고유, 추상명사

① **A professor** did the work.

② **My family** is large.

③ She had her **hair** cut.

④ I bought **a Ford** yesterday.

⑤ He was fascinated by her **beauty.**

4. 명사류: 명사, 대명사, 동명사, 부정사, 명사절

① **Korea** is famous for its beautiful scenery.

② **He** finally passed the driver's license examination.

③ I am considering **buying a car.**

④ He works hard **to pass the exam.**

⑤ It is true **that he is honest.**

Unit 02 불가산명사

1. 불가산명사는 부정관사 사용 불가, 복수 불가, 복수동사 불가, 단수 취급

종류	예시
물질명사	water, coffee, tea, air, salt
추상명사	beauty, courage, hatred, information, advice
고유명사	Seoul, Daegu, Busan, Jeong Bok Lee

2. 시험에 잘 나오는 불가산 명사들

equipment, furniture, money, advice, information, baggage/luggage, scenery, news, mail

① He has a lot of information about Canada.

② The company doesn't produce much machinery in Vietnam.

Unit 03 가산명사

1. 가산명사는 반드시 한정사가 붙거나, 그렇지 않으면 복수형을 만들어야 한다.

한정사란?

a(n), the, 소유격, another, this, that, these, those, each, every, some, any

2. 빈출 가산명사

① **눈에 보이는 것**, 만질 수 있는 사람/사물은 가산명사

② 특히 빈출, **사람을 지칭하는 단어들**은 모두 가산

③ **시간** 관련(day, week, month, year)도 가산

④ **서류** 관련(report, statement, proposal, estimate 등)은 모두 가산

⑤ **보여주기**(show, exhibition, region, map 등) 관련도 모두 가산

⑥ **규칙** 관련(regulations, standards, codes, directions, steps, procedures, measures 등)

⑦ **증가/감소** 관련(뒤에는 in)

   an increase, a hike, a jump, a rise,

   a decrease, a reduction, a decline, a drop

⑧ **돈과 관련된 것은 모두 가산명사**

   refund, price, account, credit card, bank, cost, bill,

   salary, benefit, bonus, wage, revenue, income, profit

3. 참고: 가산, 불가산이 바뀌면서 뜻이 바뀌는 단어들

business: 회사(C), 사업(U)

room: 방(C), 공간(U)

notice: 통지서(C), 통지(U)

condition: 조건(C), 상태(U)

Unit 04 복합명사

1. 명사는 두 번 오면 안 되는 것이 원칙, 앞에 있는 명사를 형용사 취급

address verification 주소지 확인

baggage allowance 수하물 중량 제한

building expansion 건물 확장

project manager 프로젝트 매니저

customer (client) satisfaction 고객 만족

money management 돈 관리

application form 신청서, 지원서

business sense 사업 감각

complaint form 항의 양식 문서

parking lot 주차장

replacement fee 교체 비용

2. 단, 예외적으로 앞에 복수형을 쓰는 것도 있다.

customs office 세관

electronics company 전자 회사

savings bank 저축 은행

sales manager 판매 부장

sports complex 종합 경기장

CheckUp 2. Select the best answer to complete each sentence.

1. I need to buy a (plane's ticket, plane ticket).

2. I'm going to buy some flowers. There is a (flower, flowers) shop.

Unit 05 소유격

1. 생물의 소유격: 's를 붙인다. 다만 복수명사는 발음상 apostrophe만 사용

ex. students'

2. 무생물의 소유격: 명사와 명사 사이에 of를 사용

cf. 다만, 기간, 거리, 가격, 무게의 명사는 무생물이지만, apostrophe를 사용

Unit 06 사람명사와 사물명사의 구별

advising/advisor, attendance/attendee, interviewing/interviewer,

assembly/assembler, campaign/campaigner, rivalry/rival,

presidency/president, account/accountant, membership/members

CheckUp 2. Select the best answer to complete each sentence.

1. The new (assistance, assistant) takes care of cleaning the office early in the morning.

2. New (investments, investors) will visit the branch in Hong Kong.

Practice Test A

☑️ 다음 빈칸에 가장 적절한 것을 고르시오.

1) She arrived here with _____.
(A) some baggage
(B) a few baggage
(C) much baggage
(D) lots of baggages

2) He shoed me _____ a few days ago.
(A) some his father's books
(B) his father's some books
(C) his father's books of some
(D) some books of his father's

3) _____ of money has been spent on the project.
(A) Many
(B) The number
(C) A large number
(D) A great deal

4) _____ were at the reception.
(A) Only few person
(B) Only a few person
(C) Only few people
(D) Only a few people

5) Can you make change for _____?
(A) twenty-dollar bill
(B) a twenty-dollar bill
(C) twenty-dollars bill
(C) a twenty-dollars bill

6) _____ more expensive than flour.
(A) Bread is   (B) Bread are   (C) Breads is   (D) Breads are

7) _____ birds of a feather flock together.
(A) A   (B) An   (C) The   (D) ∅

8) _____ has been played for religious ceremonies for a long time.
(A) A music   (B) The music   (C) Music   (D) Musics

9) In Britain, Mother's Day is _____ in May.
(A) a fourth Sunday
(B) the fourth Sunday
(C) fourth Sunday
(D) four Sunday

10) _____ China's official name is _____ People's Republic of China.
(A) ∅, the   (B) the, the   (C) the, ∅   (D) ∅, ∅

Practice Test B

1) I appreciate your _____ about this matter.
(A) sensitive   (B) sensible   (C) sensitivity   (D) senses

2) Two methods of _____ can be used when you buy a product in a department store.
(A) pay   (B) payment   (C) payer   (D) payable

3) He felt _____ rise in him at the news.
(A) a patriot   (B) patriot   (C) one patriot   (D) the patriot

4) _____ of job performance usually takes place at the end of the week.
(A) Reviewed   (B) Reviewer   (C) Review   (D) Reviews

5) The company accepted _____ for those defective products.
(A) responsibility (B) responsible   (C) response   (D) to response

6) A language institute is looking for an _____ to teach an accounting course.
(A) instruct   (B) instructive   (C) instruction   (D) instructor

7) For advice about how to get a job, please talk to our experienced _____.
(A) consult   (B) consultant   (C) consultation   (D) consulting

8) Employees in the payroll department gave their _____ to the charity last week.
(A) donate   (B) donations   (C) donator   (D) to donate

9) We tried to handle the fragile items with _____ when they were delivered.
(A) cautious   (B) caution   (C) cautiously   (D) cautioned

10) We really would like to get _____ about the traffic accident.
(A) some information   (B) an information
(C) informations   (D) plenty of informations

Practice Test C

☑ 밑줄 친 부분 중 어법상 어색한 곳을 고르시오.

1) The price of <u>all these items</u> <u>are</u> two <u>hundred</u> and twenty <u>dollars</u>.
              A   B   C   D

2) <u>Only one</u> of the students <u>are going to</u> <u>major in</u> physics <u>in university</u>.
   A   B   C   D

3) Did you hear <u>many</u> news about the <u>economic</u> situation in Korea <u>while</u> you
              A   B   C
were <u>in</u> Canada?
    D

4) Every <u>animal</u> and plant <u>need</u> clean air and <u>water</u> <u>to survive</u>.
         A   B   C   D

5) <u>There are</u> <u>two kind</u> of <u>living</u> things in the world; animals and <u>plants</u>.
   A   B   C   D

6) We will need <u>only a few</u> food for <u>the picnic</u> because <u>others</u> will prepare
                A   B   C
<u>their</u> own.
   D

7) The committee <u>adhere</u> to <u>its</u> decision <u>to limit</u> <u>the evidence</u>.
              A   B   C   D

8) <u>The United States</u> Navy has studied the <u>possible</u> <u>of having</u> people <u>live</u>
       A   B   C   D
beneath the ocean.

9) Mr. Cohen looks <u>like</u> <u>a</u> unhappy person, and his wife <u>looks</u> <u>stubborn</u>.
                A B   C   D

10) <u>The highest</u> mountain <u>in the world</u> is <u>the Mount Everest</u>, which is located
     A   B   C
in <u>Nepal</u> and is 29, 141 feet high.
     D

Reading Comprehension

Questions 1-4 refer to the following e-mail.

You are 1._____ requested to acknowledge this e-mail. May we remind
you that our terms of trade are 30 days and that goods are supplied on the
understanding of payment by the 2._____ time. May we remind you for
the third time that this account is 3._____ for payment. It is essential
that the necessary steps be taken to settle this account 4._____.

1. (A) kindness   (B) kind
   (C) unkind   (D) kindly

2. (A) fair   (B) proper
   (C) careful   (D) likely

3. (A) overdue   (B) overworked
   (C) overran   (D) overcharged

4. (A) costly   (B) frequently
   (C) immediately   (D) recently

Questions 5-7 refer to the following article.

In Europe, the average number of working hours per week ranges from 42.2 hours in Greece to 37.9 hours in Sweden. This is in contrast to what European governments have actually agreed to with trade unions with regard to working hours. For example, the average number of working hours per week for full-time workers in France should be 35 hours. In reality, however, it's just under 40. Interestingly, although one of the reasons for the 35-hour workweek in France was to increase employment, this hasn't happened. Despite this, 39% of French companies told researchers that they expect to let their workers work four days per week in the future.

5. What is the main purpose of this article?
   (A) To announce that the working conditions are bad in Europe
   (B) To inform readers of European standards for working hours
   (C) To tell readers some differences between working hours and productivity
   (D) To notify readers of the importance of working hours

6. Which country works the longest hours in Europe?
   (A) France   (B) Sweden
   (C) Germany   (D) Greece

7. Why was the workweek in France reduced to 35 hours?
   (A) To decrease unemployment
   (B) To keep the trade unions happy
   (C) To allow workers to have a 4-day workweek
   (D) To keep up with other European countries

Self Review

✅ **명사**에 대해 아는 대로 써보세요. 그리고 다시 한번 복습하시기 바랍니다!!!

명사의 종류	
불가산명사	
가산명사	
복합명사	
소유격	
사람명사와 사물명사	

PRONOUN

Chapter 4 PRONOUN

대명사의 종류
인칭대명사(소유대명사, 재귀대명사), 지시대명사, 의문대명사, 부정대명사, 관계대명사

대명사는 말 그대로 명사를 앞, 뒤에서 대신하는 것을 말한다. 여기에는 영어가 반복을 싫어하는 언어라는 것을 알 수 있다. 여러 종류가 많으나 인칭대명사가 가장 중요하다고 할 수 있다.

Unit 01 인칭대명사

구분	주격	소유격	목적격	소유대명사	재귀대명사
1인칭 단수	I	my	me	mine	myself
2인칭 단/복수	you	your	you	yours	yourself/ yourselves
3인칭 단수	he	his	him	his	himself
	she	her	her	hers	herself
	it	its	it	x	itself
1인칭 복수	we	our	us	ours	ourselves
3인칭 복수	they	their	them	theirs	themselves

① It is easier to ask the questions than to answer **them**.

② A working mother is usually worried about **her** children.

③ His pronunciation is bad, and **my** pronunciation is too.

④ I met a friend of **mine**.

⑤ Esther has a cat and **its** name is Spike.

⑥ These books are yours and **those** are my books.

⑦ Carnegie taught **himself** how to read and write.

⑧ My grandmother wants to live in the country **by herself**.

⑨ **Nobody** knows for sure what will happen tomorrow.

⑩ There isn't **anyone** in the office.

1. 인칭대명사(주격, 소유격, 목적격)

보기 4개가 대명사로 이루어진 경우는

① **앞으로 가서** 대명사가 받아주는 명사 확인(단/복수, 사람/사물, 여자/남자)

② **뒤로 가서 격 확인**(빈칸 뒤가 동사면 **주격**, 주어+타동사면 **목적격**, 주어+자동사+전치사면 목적격, 빈칸 뒤 명사만 있으면 **소유격**)

CheckUp 1. Select the best answer to complete each sentence.

1. A bird uses (its, their) wings to fly.
2. Teachers should be supportive of (his, their) students.
3. My family is big. (It is, They are) composed of eight members.
4. (They, You) say that we can help the Earth if we all try.
5. Tom wanted to see my receipt, so I gave it to (his, him).
6. The successful businessman wants to write about (his, him) experiences in life.
7. Do not try to fix the refrigerator (myself, yourself); call a repairman.
8. Some people do not like to travel by (themselves, them).

---

2. 소유대명사 (소유격+명사) - his, father's 유의

① 소유대명사는 명사: 문장의 주, 목, 보어에 씀. 명사와 두 번 연속 안 됨

② 혼자로는 쓰이지 않음: 앞에 소유격+명사가 먼저 등장한 경우에 사용

③ **이중 소유격**: 명사의 소유격은 한정사(a, an, the. another, every, each, some, any, no 등과 같이 나란히 쓸 수 없음)

CheckUp 2. Select the best answer to complete each sentence.

1. He is (a my friend, a friend of mine).
2. He is (a my father's friend, a friend of my father's).

---

3. 재귀 대명사

① 재귀적 용법: 동사나 전치사의 목적어가 행위 주체와 같은 경우(생략하면 문장 성립 안 됨)

해법: 행위 주체를 찾아 −self를 붙여 줌

숙어: by oneself 혼자, for oneself 혼자 힘으로, of oneself 저절로

② 강조적 용법: 문장의 주어, 목적어, 보어로 쓰인 명사와 동격일 때(생략해도 문장 성립)

해법: 동격의 그 명사를 받아서 −self를 붙여준다.

Unit 02 It과 지시대명사

it, this, that, these, those

1. It의 용법

종류	예문
인칭대명사 (앞 명사/ 앞 구문)	앞 명사: He gave me a present. It was a book. 앞 구문: He tried to solve the problem, but it was impossible.
비인칭 주어 (시간, 날씨, 거리, 요일, 상황)	시간: It's two o'clock now. 날씨: It's raining now. 거리: It's 10km from my school to my house. 요일: It's Sunday. Will you go to the movies with me? 상황: How is it with your business?
가주어 (부정사, that절)	부정사: It is difficult to master English. that절: It is true that he is honest.
가목적어 (부정사, that절)	부정사: I found it difficult to master English. that절: He took it for granted that I helped her.
강조구문 (It ~ that S+V)	주어 강조: It was I that met her in the park yesterday. 목적어 강조: It was her that I met in the park yesterday. 장소 강조: It was in the park that I met her yesterday. 시간 강조: It was yesterday that I met her in the park.

2. 지시대명사

① 지시대명사: 주어, 목적어, 보어 자리에 올 수 있고 혼자서 쓰일 수 있다.

지시형용사: 명사를 수식, 단/복수를 맞춘다.

② 관사, 소유격과 함께 쓰이면 틀림

③ 빈 칸 뒤에 of가 있으면, that of, those of구문이라고 보는 게 거의 정답

④ those who~, those -ing/p.p, those 전치사+명사 (-하는 사람들)

CheckUp 3. Select the best answer to complete each sentence.

1. Korea's climate is colder than (that, those) of Taiwan.

2. (That, Those) who have worked here for five years or more will receive a bonus.

---

3. 의문사

① 의문대명사 (who(m), what, which)

② 의문형용사 (whose, what, which) -what은 범위 없고, which는 한정범위

③ 의문부사 (how, when, where, why)

* 의문사 주어+ 동사 = 의문사 to부정사 (명사 기능)

Unit 03 부정대명사

여기서 부정이란 말은 정하지 아니한 즉 불특정한 사람이나 사물을 지칭

1. one, another, some, (the) other(s)

one과 another(가장 빈출, 여러 개 중에 아무거나 하나, 또 하나)

one과 the other(하나는~ 마지막 하나는 ~)

one과 the others(많은 것 중, 하나는~, 나머지 모두는~)

some과 others(많은 것 중, 몇 개는 ~, 다른 몇 개는 ~)

some과 the others(많은 것 중, 몇 개는 ~, 나머지 모두는~)

* one : a + 명사를 대신, a beautiful one, some cute ones

CheckUp 4. Select the best answer to complete each sentence.

1. You ordered two items. One is a printer, and (another, the other) is a computer monitor.

2. There are three shipments. One is for Hong Kong, (another, other) for Vietnam, and the other for India.

3. Some members are happy with the decision, but (another, the others) are not sure about it.

4. One of the employees plays the flute. (Some, Another) plays the drums.

---

2. each other(2) / one another(3) 서로

3. one after the other / one after another 차례로

CheckUp 5. Select the best answer to complete each sentence.

1. New employees tend to help (each other, one another) to adjust to the new environment.

2. My business partner and I respect (each other, one another).

---

4. 부정대명사의 단/복수

another, the other, other가 형용사와 명사로 쓰일 때 차이점

another+가산단수명사/ +불가산명사(×)

other+복수명사/ +불가산명사(○)

the other+단수명사, 복수명사/ +불가산명사(○)

5. another + 숫자 + 복수명사(추가로 ~명)

CheckUp 6. Select the best answer to complete each sentence.

1. I have two dogs. One is black and (the other, another) is white.
2. There are four colors in the Korean flag. Two colors are black and white, (Others, The others) are red and blue.
3. Some prefer classical music, but (others, the others) prefer pop music.
4. Do you have any (other, others) books about world organizations?
5. This shirt is too tight. Could you show me (another, other) one?
6. Mr. Green has three cars. One is red, (another, the other) is white, and the third is black.
7. Jack and I have known (each other, one after another) for a long time.
8. The Olympic Games are held (every fourth year, every fourth years).

---

6. "대부분"이란 뜻의 부정대명사

most of the 명사, most 명사, almost all of the 명사, almost all the 명사

* 가산, 불가산 모두 가능

cf. 유사 표현: one, either, both, few, many of the 복수 가산명사

none, half, some/any, all of the 가산/불가산명사 모두

7. 부정대명사 any vs. some

① any는 의문문, 부정문, 조건문에, some은 긍정문에 쓰는 것이 원칙

② 둘 다 대명사와 형용사 기능 가능

any, some + 가산단수명사, 가산복수명사, 불가산명사

any, some of the 가산복수명사, 불가산명사

③ any는 부정문에서는 주어로는 사용 안된다. (주어자리의 any는 no로)

Anybody cannot solve the problem. (×)

Nobody can solve the problem. (○)

→ The problem can be solved by nobody. (×)

→ The problem cannot be solved by anybody. (○)

④ any가 긍정문에 사용되는 경우도 있다(어떤 ~라도)

CheckUp 7. Select the best answer to complete each sentence.

1. People waited in line all day for the concert tickets. (Some, Any) were disappointed.

2. The teacher offered to answer questions, but no one had (some, any).

8. 부정어 정리

① few +가산복수명사, little+불가산명사 (두 단어 모두, 형/명사 다 됨)

② none 대명사: 가산/불가산, 사람/사물 모두 대용

no 형용사: 가산, 불가산 명사와 사용(no +명사 = not any 명사)

not 부사: v, a 수식, not all 부분부정

I have not a friend.

I have no friend.

I have none.

③ nothing: 대명사

④ 기타 대명사 either, neither, both: 형용사, 명사로도 사용

Practice Test A

☑ 다음 빈칸에 가장 적절한 것을 고르시오.

1) Every culture _____ styles and traditions of singing.
(A) has its own (B) have its own
(C) has their own (D) have their own

2) I have three brothers, _____ is a doctor, _____ a teacher, and the third
   a businessman.
(A) one − other (B) one − another
(C) one − the other (D) the one − the other

3) All of you should think long and hard about _____ before choosing a job.
(A) you (B) your (C) yourself (D) yourselves

4) Our parents worry about my sister more than _____.
(A) I (B) me (C) my (D) myself

5) _____ to be laughed at by others.
(A) One like (B) No one like (C) None likes (D) No one likes

6) The team is preparing for _____.
(A) its big game (B) it's big game
(C) their big game (D) theirs big game

7) Some like cream and sugar in their coffee, while _____ like it black.
(A) another (B) other (C) others (D) the others

8) Students should do _____.
(A) his best (B) your best (C) their best (D) theirs best

9) The World Cup Soccer Games are held _____.
(A) every four year (B) every four years
(C) every fourth year (D) every fourth years

10) Some of the English teachers are from the U.S., and _____ from Canada.
(A) other (B) others (C) the other (D) the others

Practice Test B

1) I can't write the final report until _____ finish collecting the data.
(A) they   (B) their   (C) them   (D) theirs

2) Why don't you use my laptop if _____ doesn't work well?
(A) it   (B) I   (C) you   (D) yours

3) Although the staff has grown, Ms. Yang keeps conducting all meetings
_____.
(A) she   (B) her   (C) hers   (D) herself

4) One new product was released last month, and _____ will be put on the
market in December.
(A) any   (B) other   (C) all   (D) another

5) Only two of the applicants got interviewed. _____ didn't earn the chance.
(A) Those   (B) The others   (C) Others   (D) All

6) Please remove keys and coins from your pockets if you have _____.
(A) some   (B) each   (C) any   (D) this

7) _____ of the tourists bought a ticket before getting on the shuttle bus.
(A) Each   (B) Every   (C) This   (D) That

8) _____ that the formation of the sun began with the condensation of an
interstellar gas cloud.
(A) Believing   (B) To believe   (C) The belief   (D) It is believed

9) The use of radar _____ for the police to intercept most speeders.
(A) makes it possibility   (B) makes it possible
(C) makes possible   (D) makes possibility

10) Is the climate of Italy _____?
(A) similar like Florida   (B) somewhat similar to Florida
(C) so much like Florida   (D) somewhat like that of Florida

Practice Test C

☑ 밑줄 친 부분 중 어법상 어색한 곳을 고르시오.

1) When Amundsen <u>made</u> his plan to sail to <u>the</u> Arctic, <u>she</u> spent <u>a lot of</u>
                 A   B   C   D
money getting ready and owed money to many people.

2) If she <u>borrows</u> <u>your</u> book, then you should <u>be able to</u> borrow <u>her</u>.
          A   B   C   D

3) <u>All the</u> students <u>are working</u> <u>late</u> tonight to finish <u>his</u> reports.
  A   B   C   D

4) If a person really <u>wants</u> to succeed, <u>they</u> should <u>always</u> work <u>hard</u>.
                  A   B   C   D

5) Yesterday the teacher <u>spoke to</u> <u>both of us</u>, <u>Tom and I</u>, about <u>our</u> test
                       A   B   C   D
record.

6) All <u>living</u> creatures <u>pass on</u> inherited traits <u>from</u> one generation to <u>other</u>.
     A   B   C   D

7) When I lost <u>my</u> passport, I <u>had to</u> apply <u>the</u> another <u>one</u>.
             A   B   C   D

8) <u>A political</u> leader should have the ability <u>to adapt</u> <u>themselves</u> to a <u>changing</u>
   A   B   C   D
<u>world</u>.

9) Rachel and <u>her</u> husband <u>have known</u> <u>one after another</u> since they <u>were</u>
             A   B   C   D
children.

10) <u>In 1947</u>, India gained <u>their</u> independence <u>from Britain</u>, but the country <u>was</u>
    A   B   C
<u>split</u> into mainly Hindu India and mainly Muslim Pakistan.
   D

Reading Comprehension

Questions 1-4 refer to the following notice.

From: Mason Brown, Head of Department
       Marketing and Sales
To: Jerry Cooper, Field Worker
       Financial Services
Date: October 20, 2006

This notice is written confirmation that I am providing you with an opportunity to improve your performance to a 1._____ level. I have determined that your performance is unacceptable in two 2._____ areas of your work, and therefore, a performance improvement plan is required. The plan outlines activities that you must complete to improve your performance. If you have any concerns about the plan or require 3._____ guidance, please let me know as soon as possible. The plan becomes 4._____ today and will continue for 35 days.

1. (A) better   (B) sooner
     (C) worse   (D) less

2. (A) criticize   (B) criticizes
     (C) criticizing   (D) critical

3. (A) addition   (B) addictive
     (C) additional   (D) additionally

4. (A) effectively   (B) effective
     (C) affectively   (D) affective

Questions 5-7 refer to the following article.

Despite e-mail and the Internet, business people actually spend more time than ever going to and from meetings. In Silicon Valley, it is estimated that $3.5 billion is wasted each year because of blocked highways caused by people who need to get into their cars and travel. One expert says that he spends 75% of his time on the road. The number of people crossing time zones is estimated to be 20 million worldwide, and this number is likely to double by 2010.

5. Why is $3.5 billion wasted in Silicon Valley each year?
   (A) Because of heavy traffic and severe traffic jams
   (B) Because of delays on the Internet and internet servers
   (C) Because of international flights and crossing time zones
   (D) Because of too many people being involved in the technological revolution

6. How many people will be crossing time zones in the world by 2010?
   (A) 3.5 billion   (B) 40 million
   (C) 20 million   (D) 10 million

7. According to the article, what has increased recently?
   (A) The number of car accidents
   (B) The number of people using e-mail
   (C) The number of businesses using the Internet
   (D) The number of people traveling to meetings

Self Review

☑ 대명사에 대해 아는 대로 써보세요. 그리고 다시 한번 복습하시기 바랍니다!!!

인칭대명사	
재귀대명사	
it과 지시대명사	
부정대명사	

5
chapter

AGREEMENT

Chapter 5 AGREEMENT

일치란 주어와 동사간의 단수, 복수관계를 설명하는 말이다. 단수명사 주어에는 단수동사가, 복수명사 주어에는 복수동사가 적용된다. 또한 시제 간에도 일치관계가 성립되는데 이를 시제의 일치라고 한다.

Unit 01 주어-동사 수일치

1. 동사에 밑줄이 있으면 주어를 찾아 단/복수를 확인하고, 주어에 밑줄이 있으면 동사를 찾아 단/복수를 확인하라!

(ex. The aim of these games is ...)

CheckUp 1. Select the best answer to complete each sentence.
1. Mr. White (attends, attend) conferences to improve his marketing skills.
2. The manager and his assistant (is, are) traveling to Beijing.
3. The new receptionist occasionally (makes, make) mistakes because of stress.

2. "주어+수식어구+동사" 구조에서 수식 어구를 없는 것으로 취급

수식어구의 종류 - 형용사류, 부사류

CheckUp 2. Select the best answer to complete each sentence.
1. The concert tickets which I purchased through a website (has, have) just arrived.
2. The chairs in the lobby (needs, need) to be removed.

3. 관계사절속 일치

관계사절 속의 동사도 정동사이므로, 앞의 선행명사와 단/복수 일치 필요
① My wife who lives in Daegu is very beautiful.
② The students to whom the teacher is talking are very handsome.

4. 상관 접속사는 해석법과 근접원리법을 같이 적용

① 해석법: 해석을 해보고 화자가 강조하는 바를 주어로 삼는 방법

both A and B

not A but B

not only A but also B

(=B as well as A)

② 근접원리법: 강조되는 바가 명확치 않으면 동사와 가까운 쪽을 주어로!

neither A nor B

either A or B

5. 다음 단어들이 있으면 반드시 단수명사+단수동사 사용!

a/an, another, a little/little, much, every/each, this/that, neither/either

6. 다음 단어들이 있으면 반드시 복수명사+복수동사 사용!

other, a few/few, many, both/several, these/those, various/a variety of

7. 복수/불가산명사 둘 다 적용

lots of, a lot of, plenty of, all

Unit 02 주의해야 할 수일치

1. 함께 외울 구조

① a number of +복.명+복.동

the number of+복.명+단.동

② 부분명사 of+복.명+복.동

부분명사 of+단.명+단.동

*부분명사: most, the rest, half, part, the majority, XX percent(근접원리법을 생각!)

③ one of the 복.명+단.동

several of the +복.명+복.동

④ each of the 복.명+단.동(each 단.명+단.동)

either of the 복.명+단.동(either 단.명+단.동)

neither of the 복.명+단.동(neither 단.명+단.동)

1. A number of shareholders (supports, support) the new policy.
2. A great amount of research (has, have) reviewed the market trend toward high technology.
3. Most of the employees at the factory (works, work) late almost every day.

2. 기타 주요 단/복수 Tip

① There is/are구문은 동사+주어 구조

② 국가명, 학문(-ics), 서적, 병명 등은 단수동사 및 무관사

③ 대칭형명사는 복수 취급

  (glasses, spectacles, pants, trousers, scissors, shoes, socks, stockings)

④ 동명사와 부정사, 명사절은 단수 취급

⑤ 대명사도 단/복수 일치를 참조

The United States **is** a rich country.

Mathematics **is** taught by him.

The Times **is** one of the most famous magazines in the world.

Measles **is** fatal if no early diagnosis is peformed.

cf. His mathematics are weak. (그의 수학실력)

  My politics are different from yours. (나의 정치적 견해)

  These statistics have alarmed some meteorologists. (이런 통계자료들)

3. 시간, 거리, 중량, 가격, 면적 등을 나타내는 복수명사는 단일개념으로 취급, 단수취급

Ten years is too long a time to her.

Ten dollars is too high a price for shoes.

Twenty miles is a day's journey in this valley.

Ten years have passed since he died.

A year and a half has passed since he died.

Unit 03 근접원리

동사는 근접해 있는 명사와 수를 동일하게 한다는 원리

1. Either A or B

Neither A nor B
A or B
Not only A but also B   + 동사
Not A but B
Either you or he is happy.

2. 관계대명사 선행사로서의 one of -구조

He is one of the students who have passed the exam.

3. 부분 + of the 명사(가산복수명사 + 복수동사)
부분 + of the 명사(불가산명사 + 단수동사)

part
the rest
some
any   + of + 정해진 명사 + 동사
all
most
two-thirds

All of **her money** was spent on clothes.
All of **the toys** were broken.
The rest of **the apple** is rotten.
The rest of **the apples** are rotten.
A third of **the students** were present.

Most students like to play baseball.
Most of ***students** like to baseball.
        the students
        them

4. More than +명사 +동사 구조

More than **a person** was present.

More than **two persons** were present.

5. A number(total, pair) of +복수명사 +복수동사 구조

A number of books are missing in the library.

6. 관계대명사 What절

What(**The thing** that) I want is a book.

What(**The things** that) I want are books.

Unit 04 비간섭 원리

수식어구가 있는 경우 진짜 주어에 동사를 일치시킴

1. 기본 문형

Peter, along with his brothers, plans to open a store.

The major cause of highway car accidents in 1996 was drunk drivers.

The number of books from the library is large.

Either of these hats suits you.

Neither of the answers you gave is satisfactory to us.

He is **the only one** of the students who has passed the exam.

One of the students is happy.

You as well as he are happy.

cf. A as well as B (B뿐만 아니라 A도)

　　A (together) with B (B와 함께 A가)

　　A along with B (B와 함께 A가)

　　A in addition to B (B에다 A도)

　　A besides B (B 외에 A도)

CheckUp 4. Select the best answer to complete each sentence.

1. The doctor and professor (was, were) present at the meeting.

2. Ten years (is, are) a long time to live abroad.

3. Mathematics (is, are) a difficult subject.

4. Many a person (dies, die) of cancer.

5. Two-thirds of my friends (has, have) passed the test.

6. The poor (envy, envies) the rich.

7. Every boy and girl (was, were) invited to the meeting.

8. All that (glitter, glitters) is not gold.

9. He as well as you (are, is) happy.

10. No news (is, are) good news.

11. My family (is, are) all very well.

12. The English (is, are) a practical people.

Practice Test A

다음 빈칸에 가장 적절한 것을 고르시오.

1) He made a cake last night; some of it _____ still on the table.
(A) is   (B) are   (C) had been   (D) were

2) "How is the progress?" "Two-thirds of the work _____ finished.
(A) are   (B) is   (C) to be   (D) will

3) In Virginia, the land was rich. As a result, _____ colonists were able to proper from the land and build luxurious homes.
(A) many   (B) many a   (C) many of   (D) a good deal

4) _____ of the people in our tour group were senior citizens who won a trip to England through the Rotany's annual lottery.
(A) Almost   (B) Every   (C) Most   (D) Any

5) The media has mentioned in the past months that _____ retailers will suffer financially due to a slow economy.
(A) most of   (B) most   (C) the most   (D) almost

6) _____ people living in large, polluted cities suffer from skin and respiratory diseases, which cause them to move out of the city and into the suburbs.
(A) Much   (B) Many   (C) A little   (D) Every

7) Obtaining a good job _____ difficult due to the economic situation.
(A) have remained   (B) are remaining
(C) remain   (D) remains

8) Every area manager _____ required to visit all the offices under his management once a week.
(A) is   (B) are   (C) were   (D) have

9) The cell-phone charges for local calls _____ discounted for the first month.
(A) has   (B) was   (C) is   (D) are

10) Several candidates _____ at least two foreign languages fluently.
(A) speak   (B) speaks   (C) has spoken   (D) was spoken

Practice Test B

1) Green business _____ become an expanding market because emphasis on the environment is increasing.
(A) is   (B) are   (C) has   (D) have

2) The furniture in the hotel _____ very stylish.
(A) look   (B) looks   (C) looking   (D) are

3) People who are interested in the charity event _____ to write their names on the application forms.
(A) will invite   (B) has invited   (C) was inviting   (D) are invited

4) _____ tourists from all around the world visit and enjoy the festival.
(A) Each   (B) One   (C) Many   (D) Much

5) Only one of the attendees _____ giving a presentation at the workshop.
(A) is   (B) have   (C) are   (D) has

6) Not only you but also I _____ to blame.
(A) are   (B) am   (C) has   (D) have

7) Either you or she _____ in the wrong.
(A) are   (B) am   (C) is   (D) to be

8) Ninety kilos _____ too heavy for me to lift.
(A) is   (B) are   (C) has   (D) have

9) *Crime and Punishment* _____ one of Dostoyevsky's novels.
(A) is   (B) are   (C) to be   (D) being

10) The various committees _____ now meeting to discuss your proposal.
(A) is   (B) are   (C) has   (D) have

Practice Test C

☑ 밑줄 친 부분 중 어법상 어색한 곳을 고르시오.

1) <u>Both</u> he and his wife <u>has</u> to <u>take care</u> of <u>their</u> baby.
   A   B   C   D

2) The number of <u>wild horses</u> on Assateague <u>are</u> increasing lately, <u>resulting</u> in
                 A   B   C
<u>overgrazed</u> marsh and dune grasses.
   D

3) <u>In</u> the novel, everyone <u>try</u> to <u>thwart</u> their <u>efforts</u>.
   A   B   C   D

4) The <u>survey</u> forms <u>was</u> <u>not</u> filled out <u>completely</u>.
     A   B C   D

5) The headquarters <u>and</u> the branch office <u>plans</u> <u>to reorganize</u> some <u>divisions</u>.
            A   B   C   D

6) Our facilities <u>have</u> available <u>for family</u> and <u>company</u> events <u>every</u> weekend.
        A   B   C   D

7) All <u>of</u> the old magazines <u>is</u> available <u>at</u> a <u>discounted</u> price.
   A   B   C   D

8) <u>The competition</u> <u>between</u> low-cost <u>airlines</u> <u>have</u> increased.
      A   B   C   D

9) Senior <u>employees</u> <u>in</u> the workplace <u>knows</u> less <u>about</u> computers.
      A B   C   D

10) <u>Many</u> offices <u>instructs</u> employees about <u>what to do</u> <u>in case of</u> fire.
   A   B   C   D

Reading Comprehension

Questions 1-4 refer to the following news article.

When we communicate with 1._____ we usually use words. We also use 2._____ means to communicate, sometimes more powerful than spoken language. This is called body language. Body language is a kind of communication 3._____ gestures. Most of the time, we are not aware that we are doing this. We gesture with 4._____ eyebrows ore hands. or meet someone else's eyes and look away. The researchers noted different human gestures and their possible meanings. Then they sorted them into different patterns according to the culture in which they are used.

1. (A) other
   (C) worse
   (B) another
   (D) the other

2. (A) neither
   (C) each
   (B) another
   (D) each other

3. (A) which
   (C) so
   (B) what
   (D) as

4. (A) we
   (C) ours
   (B) us
   (D) our

Questions 5-9 refer to the following review and letter.

"Cowboy Cop" Lacks Sens

By Trisha Einsten

"Cowboy Cop" was a poorly done movie that did not live up to any of the hype. As a comedy, "Cowboy Cop" relied too much on sight gags and slapstick. The movie also had no romance.

The acting was decent, and Lee Gorman gives a surprisingly good performance as Sheriff Gentry. In one scene, Gorman goes to a bank to withdraw some money and walks in during a bank robbery. He quickly foils the bank robber, while saving a little boy from being harmed.

Overall, the movie is slow and boring. I would wait until this comes out on DVD before watching it.

Dear Ms, Einsten,

I just read your interview of Cowboy Cop, and I must say that I disagree 100 percent. Although I agree that the movie lacks romance, it is a comedy. Some of the slapstick is the best I've seen in a movie all year. Lee Gorman is an awesome cop, and the scene in the café is worth the price of admission by itself. I really think you should re-evaluate your stand on this movie.

Sincerely,
Meg Wharton
Meg Wharton

---

5. Why does Lee Gorman go into the bank?
(A) To save a little boy
(B) To withdraw some money
(C) To foil a bank robber
(D) To rob it

6. When does the reviewer think you should watch this movie?
(A) When it comes out on DVD
(B) When it comes out on video
(C) Sometime this year
(D) After you re-evaluate your stand

7. What kind of movie Cowboy Cop?

(A) A romantic comedy　　　　　(B) A love story

(C) A science fiction　　　　　(D) A comedy

8. How does the reviewer describe the movie?

(A) Fast paced and funny　　　　(B) Slow, with plenty of romance

(C) Slow and tedious　　　　　(D) Perfect for the whole family

9. What does Meg Wharton think of Lee Gorman?

(A) He is very good.　　　　　(B) He is stiff.

(C) He is bad.　　　　　　　(D) He is funny.

Self Review

☑️ **일치**에 대해 아는 대로 써보세요. 그리고 다시 한번 복습하시기 바랍니다!!!

주어-동사 수일치	
주의해야 할 수일치	
근접원리	
비간섭원리	

MEMO

ADJECTIVE

Chapter 6 ADJECTIVE

형용사는 크게 문법 문제와 뜻을 묻는 문제로 볼 수 있다. 문법은 명사를 앞/뒤에서 수식하는 기능과 보어 역할을 한다. 그리고 명사와 같이 사용되는 형용사의 기능에 유의하고 어순에 신경을 쓴다.

Unit 01 형용사의 역할

1. 형용사의 역할

원래 형용사는 명사를 수식함이 기본임. 주로 가산/불가산 명사와 묶어서 복수랑 어울리는 형용사, 단수랑 써야하는 형용사에 관한 출제가 자주 됨

2. 형용사가 답이 되는 4가지 경우

① be동사+(부사)+형용사

② 관사/소유격+(형용사)+명사

③ 형용사+복수명사

④ 형+형+명사, 형, 형 명사, 형 and 형 명사

* 형용사가 뒤에서 꾸밀 때: three miles away, 10 years old, ~thing/body/one ~abe/~ible등

CheckUp 1. Select the best answer to complete each sentence.

1. Vena is a (careful, carefully) driver. She always drives (careful, carefully).

2. Ted didn't do very (good, well) on his exam.

3. Rain water was once considered to be (good, well) for the complexion.

4. It is (terrible, terribly) cold today.

5. Jane is studying physics (hard, hardly), but she can (hard, hardly) understand it.

6. You are (late, lately) again. Why are you lazy (late, lately)?

7. My brother (completely forgot, forgot completely) my birthday.

8. I (have never, never have) been to China.

9. It seemed (impossible, impossibly) for the company to make a large profit this year.

10. Companies often want their employees to come up with something (innovative, innovatively)

Unit 02 수/양 형용사와 여러 형용사의 기능

1. "수"형용사 뒤에는 가산 명사 복수, "양"형용사 뒤에는 불가산 명사 단수

① 수형용사: many, a (large, good, great) number of, a great many,
　　　　　　 few, a few, not a few, quite a few
　　　　　　 both, several

* 단수: every, each(respective는 복수), another, either, neither

② 양형용사: much, a great deal of, a good deal of, a large amount of,
　　　　　　 a little, little, not a little, quite a little　　　　.

③ 양쪽 다: some/any, a lot of/lots of/plenty of, most, all,
　　　　　 부분명사: percent, half, majority, 분수

CheckUp 2. Select the best answer to complete each sentence.

1. The workers need to work late for (a few, a little) nights.
2. We need (many, much) creative ideas to win the competition.

---

2. Every의 형용사적 용법

① every +단수명사 +단수동사
② every+서수/기수/other/few+명사 "~마다, 매~"

3. 수량 형용사(hundred, thousand, million, score, dozen등)

① 막연한 수 일 때 "hundreds of"
② 정확한 수 일 때 "two hundred+명사"

4. high/low 수식 vs large, small 수식

① high/low의 수식만 되는 명사들: price, level, quality, productivity
　(price 제외, 아래는 모두 돈 관련)
② high/low, large/small의 수식이 모두 가능: cost, demand, income, profit, salary

5. "so 형/부 that" Vs. "such 명사 that"
"so 형 a +명사" Vs. "such (a) 형 +명"

She is so beautiful that everyone likes her.
She is so beautiful a girl that everyone likes her.
She is such a beautiful that everyone likes her.

Unit 03 의미상 혼동하기 쉬운 형용사

respectable 존경할만한 respectful 공손한 respective 각각의	imaginative 상상력이 풍부한 imaginable 상상할 수 있는 imaginary 가상의
sensible 지각 있는 sensitive 민감한 sensuous 감각적인 sensual 육체적인	momentary 순간적인 momentous 중요한
economic 경제의 economical 절약하는	historic 역사적으로 유명한 historical 역사에 관한
credible 믿을만한 credulous 잘 속는	considerable 상당한 considerate 사려깊은
industrial 산업의 industrious 근면한, 성실한	successful 성공한 successive 연속적인
beneficial 유익한 beneficent 친절한	negligent 태만한 negligible 하찮은
desirable 바람직한 desirous 바라는	complementary 보충의 complimentary 칭찬의
intelligent 지적인 intelligible 이해할 수 있는	portable 휴대용의 potable 마실 수 있는

Practice Test A

✔ 다음 빈칸에 가장 적절한 것을 고르시오.

1) The decision of the government was _____.
(A) shocked   (B) shocking   (C) shock   (D) the shock of

2) More and more people became _____ about our environment.
(A) concerned   (B) concerning   (C) concern   (D) the concern of

3) The Animal Farm, written by George O'Well, is popular and _____ today.
(A) appealed   (B) appealing   (C) appeal   (D) the appeal

4) _____ Heather say that again.
(A) Never will   (B) Never do   (C) Never is   (D) Never have

5) Our test results were _____ because we all did _____ on the test.
(A) good – good   (B) good – well   (C) well – good   (D) well – well

6) This computer has more functions, and it is _____ that one.
(A) twice more expensive than   (B) more twice expensive than
(C) as twice expensive as   (D) two times as expensive as

7) In my opinion, Vancouver is _____ the world.
(A) most beautiful city of   (B) the beautifulest city in
(C) the most beautiful city of   (D) the most beautiful city in

8) The greater the demand, _____.
(A) the price is high   (B) high is the price
(C) the higher the price   (D) the higher the price is

9) If you need _____ information, please ask.
(A) farther   (B) further   (C) more far   (D) farer

10) Physics is _____.
(A) one of the hardest subject   (B) one of the hardest subjects
(C) one of the most hardly subject   (D) one of the most hardly subjects

Practice Test B

1) Toru Inc. will keep its customers' personal information _____.
(A) secure   (B) securely   (C) securing   (D) security

2) The new employee earned the _____ trust of his supervisor by working hard.
(A) completed   (B) completing   (C) complete   (D) completely

3) Your team has shown _____ improvement over the past year.
(A) few   (B) a few   (C) many   (D) a lot of

4) Jane has such _____ skin that she gets burned very easily in the sun.
(A) sense   (B) sensible   (C) sensitive   (D) sensational

5) The newly established furniture store enjoyed a _____ increase in its sales volume last quarter.
(A) considerate   (B) considering   (C) considered   (D) considerable

6) Quite often, cheap products are just as good as more _____ ones.
(A) expensive   (B) routine   (C) constant   (D) affordable

7) The power plant developed a(n) _____ technique for reducing costs.
(A) attentive   (B) defective   (C) effective   (D) orderly

8) Job seekers need to be _____ with computer software such as Microsoft Word.
(A) attractive   (B) familiar   (C) popular   (D) satisfactory

9) This model comes in _____ shapes and sizes.
(A) complicated   (B) definite   (C) various   (D) valuable

10) Due to the _____ storm, many homes are still without electricity.
(A) pleased   (B) defective   (C) secure   (D) recent

Practice Test C

☑️ 밑줄 친 부분 중 어법상 어색한 곳을 고르시오.

1) There <u>is</u> a <u>specially</u> program <u>on television</u> <u>this</u> evening.
      A   B   C   D

2) After she <u>drank</u> the chocolate milk, <u>the cake</u> tasted too <u>sweetly</u> <u>to her</u>.
             A   B   C   D

3) After <u>the earthquake,</u> <u>a lot of</u> volunteers <u>were sent</u> to the <u>damaging</u> areas.
               A   B   C   D

4) <u>The students</u> thought <u>that</u> it was a <u>bored</u> topic <u>to discuss</u> in their class.
      A   B   C   D

5) The homeless usually <u>has</u> great <u>difficulty</u> in <u>getting a job</u>, so they are
                      A   B   C

losing <u>their hope</u>.
        D

6) It is <u>interested</u> that space could <u>be reached</u> in 2 hours <u>at the speed</u> of a
          A   B   C

normal car if the car <u>were</u> to drive straight upwards.
                    D

7) Professor Johnson <u>checked</u> my report <u>correctly</u> <u>more</u> <u>than</u> Professor Smith
                       A   B   C

<u>did</u>.
 D

8) <u>The summer</u> of Japan is <u>a little</u> hotter <u>than</u> <u>Korea</u>.
      A   B   C   D

9) Never <u>did</u> Mr. Williams <u>thought</u> Jennifer <u>to be</u> such <u>a good</u> woman.
        A   B   C   D

10) Seoul is one of <u>the biggest</u> <u>city</u> in <u>the world</u>, and Tokyo is <u>too</u>.
                  A   B   C   D

Reading Comprehension

Questions 1–4 refer to the following news report.

1._____ is difficult to escape the influence of television. If you fit the statistical averages, by the age of 20 2._____ will have been exposed to at least 20,000 hours of television. The only things Americans do more than watch television are work and sleep. The trouble with television is that 3._____ discourages concentration. Almost anything interesting and rewarding in life requires some constructive effort. All of us can achieve things that seem miraculous to those 4._____ never concentrate on anything. But television does not encourage us to apply any effort.

---

1. (A) It   (B) One
   (C) That   (D) Its

2. (A) he   (B) you
   (C) one   (D) they

3. (A) which   (B) one
   (C) the one   (D) it

4. (A) whoever   (B) which
   (C) who   (D) whom

Questions 5-9 refer to the following two reports.

Springfield Rated Worst City to Live In

The Jacobs Group has rated Springfield the worst city in the United States to call home. In a survey of over 300 communities with a population of over 50,000, Springfield came in dead last. Pollution, low job growth, and a lack of public parks were the main reasons given. "Springfield has seen the number of jobs decrease gradually over the last five years," said Peter Jacobs, head of the Jacobs Group. Springfield's unemployment rate stood at 7.9 percent last year, about twice as high as the national average. Longtime Springfield resident John Taylor said he has been looking for work for over a year. "I love Springfield, but right now it's tough to live here," Taylor said.

Springfield Mayor Blasts Jacobs Group Report

Springfield Mayor Paul Hagerty ripped into a report by the Jacobs Group, calling its naming of Springfield as America's worst city to live in "ridiculous." "Springfield is an open, family-oriented city," Hagerty said. Hagerty said that Springfield's education system was second to none, and that, although Springfield's unemployment rate is admittedly too high, it is beginning to fall.

Hagerty also said Springfield has some nice parks outside the city and that Springfield is clean. "To call Springfield a dirty city is not only a lie, but irresponsible and outrageous," Hagerty said.

---

5. What is NOT a reason given for naming Springfield the worst city to live in?
(A) Pollution
(B) The unemployment rate
(C) The lack of public parks
(D) The lack of good schools

6. How long has John Taylor been looking for work?
(A) Three months
(B) Six months
(C) Over a year
(D) About one year

7. How does Mayor Paul Hagerty describe Springfield?

(A) A dirty and polluted city

(B) An open, family-oriented city

(C) A city with a high unemployment rate

(D) A city with too few parks

8. The word "decrease" in paragraph 1, line 5 is closest in meaning to

(A) reduce   (B) increase

(C) open   (D) expand

9. How does John Taylor describe life in Springfield right now?

(A) An absolute pleasure   (B) Tough

(C) Not very pleasant   (D) Fun and enjoyable

Self Review

☑ **형용사에 대해 아는 대로 써보세요. 그리고 다시 한번 복습하시기 바랍니다!!!**

형용사의 역할	
수/양 형용사	
혼동하기 쉬운 형용사	

7 chapter

ADVERB

Chapter 7 ADVERB

Unit 01 부사의 역할과 위치

1. 부사는 동사, 형용사, 부사, 문장전체를 수식

CheckUp 1. Select the best answer to complete each sentence.

1. The presenter (repeated, repeatedly) stressed diligence as the best quality for a supervisor.
2. (Final, Finally), the company announced that it had decided to invest more money in the Chinese market.

---

2. 위치(완전한 문장속에서 존재)

① 동사 앞/뒤

② 조동사와 원.동 사이

③ be+-ing/pp 사이

④ to 부정사의 사이

⑤ have pp 사이

⑥ 형용사 앞

⑦ 문장 맨 앞(presumably, regrettably, actually, recently)이나, 맨 뒤

CheckUp 2. Select the best answer to complete each sentence.

1. He (still, yet) doesn't understand the assignment.
2. When I got there, Mike had (already, still) left for the airport.
3. The review for the new item in the market is (much, very) encouraging.
4. It is not (never, usually) OK to arrive at the office after 9, but it is today.

---

3. 숫자 (형용사) 앞에 잘 들어가는 지정 부사들(ad + 숫자 + 명사)

① 거의: almost, nearly, approximately, roughly, around, about

② 최대/최소: a maximum of 숫자 = up to 숫자/a minimum of 숫자

③ ~마다: every

④ 겨우: only

Unit 02 주요 부사의 어순

1. too much+명사, much(=far) too+형용사

ex. too much cost, too much sugar, much too expensive

2. 너무 ~해서 ~할 수 없다.

too a/ad to원동 (too는 부사)

He is too tired to get up early.

= He is so tired that he can't get up early.

3. enough +명사 or 형/부 enough to 원형

충분히 ~해서 ~할 수 있다.

He has enough money to buy the car.

He is old enough to go to school.

= He is so old that he can go to school.

Unit 03 혼동되는 부사

구분	품사	문장
still	부사: 여전히(현재, 현재진행 중) 부사: 그러나	주로 긍정문에 부정문에 쓴다면, "still not"
yet	부사: 아직(일어나지 않은 일) 접속사: 그러나(S+V yet S+V)	주로 부정문 "not yet" 숙어: have yet to (아직~아니다)
once	부사: 한때, 언젠가(S ad V) 접속사: 일단~하면	부사라면 동사 수식! 접속사라면 뒤에 주동 . 주동 (시제 주의)
besides	접속부사: 게다가 전치사: 게다가	접속부사:"Besides," 아니면 ",besides," 전치사라면: besides+명사
just	부사: 이제 막~ just before직전/just after직후	have just p.p 이제 막~했다. just~when ~하려고 했을 때 막 just as~as 딱~만큼 ~한
ever	부사: 언젠가	hardly ever 거의 ~ 않는다. (부정어) have ever p.p 언젠가~한적 있다. ever since 그 이래로 언젠가
already	부사: 이미, 벌써	긍정문: 완료시제와 사용 have already p.p 이미 ~했다.

1. "거의 ~하지 않다" hardly, scarcely, seldom, rarely

① not , never 와 사용 불가 (이 자체가 부정어이므로)

② 어순 : be/조동사 뒤, 일반 동사 앞

③ 특히, hardly는 hardly ever의 형태로 빈출

2. 형태상 혼동되는 부사들

① hard ad. 열심히, a. 어려운   hardly ad. 거의 ~아니다.

② near ad. 가까이에 a. 가까운   nearly ad. 거의 (+숫자)

③ high ad. 높이 a. 높은   highly ad. 매우 (highly successful)

④ late ad. 늦게 a. 작고한, 늦은   lately ad. 최근에 (recently)

3. 형용사와 형태가 같은 부사

① fast a. 빠른 ad. 빠르게

② early a./ad. 이른, 일찍

③ long a. 긴 ad. 오랫동안

④ far a. 먼 ad. 멀리

4. 다양한 형태의 부사들

① 정도부사: heavily 지나치게, badly 몹시, well below/over, well ahead of, well in advance

② 초점부사: only, even, just, exactly, particularly, especially

③ 동조부사: also 문장 중간, too 긍정문 맨 뒤, either 부정문 맨 뒤

Practice Test A

✅ 다음 빈칸에 가장 적절한 것을 고르시오.

1) They have certainly studied _____ to pass the test.
(A) hard enough   (B) hardly enough
(C) enough hard   (D) enough hardly

2) He made a presentation very _____ at the annual conference.
(A) hesitate   (B) hesitant   (C) hesitantly   (D) hesitation

3) He is a _____ efficient employee in the human resources division
(A) high   (B) highly   (C) higher   (D) height

4) The doctor _____ recommended the healthy diet to the patient.
(A) strong   (B) strength   (C) strengthen   (D) strongly

5) _____, our company didn't get the contract for some reason.
(A) Unfortune   (B) Unfortunately
(C) Unfortunate   (D) Misfortune

6) I went _____.
(A) to school everyday slowly   (B) to school slowly everyday
(C) slowly everyday to school   (D) slowly to school everyday

7) Dinner is ready; let's go _____.
(A) downstairs   (B) to downstairs (C) downstair   (D) to downstair

8) She _____ experience in her diary.
(A) usually writes down her   (B) writes usually down her
(C) writes down usually her   (D) usually her writes down

9) The seminar began _____ after the manager left the office.
(A) briefly   (B) shortly   (C) sooner   (D) rightly

10) The venture company launched the _____ designed product.
(A) renewal   (B) never   (C) newly   (D) new

Practice Test B

1) This new way of communication is _____ popular with the younger generation.
(A) increase
(B) increasing
(C) increased
(D) increasingly

2) You must examine the employment agreement _____ carefully before you sign.
(A) extreme
(B) extremely
(C) extremeness
(D) extremity

3) I had a brief talk with the CEO _____ before he left on a business trip.
(A) shortly
(B) short
(C) shorten
(D) shorts

4) The employer has not responded to the labor union _____.
(A) already
(B) yet
(C) still
(D) much

5) Companies in the technology market are competing _____ fiercely that a start-up company must be well prepared.
(A) very
(B) so
(C) too
(D) much

6) Louisa _____ ever misses a work deadline.
(A) hard
(B) hardly
(C) hardness
(D) harden

7) There have been a lot of complaints about Sarah's performance _____.
(A) late
(B) lately
(C) latter
(D) last

8) _____, local firms are relocating because of the heavy tax rates in this county.
(A) Approximately
(B) Finally
(C) Independently
(D) Increasingly

9) The staff did not _____ account for lost or stolen goods when they took inventory.
(A) considerably
(B) slightly
(C) accurately
(D) formally

10) Pitt, Briggs & Co. is seeking a new supplier because its current one is _____ late in shipping their orders.
(A) entirely
(B) rapidly
(C) consistently
(D) promptly

Practice Test C

☑ 밑줄 친 부분 중 어법상 어색한 곳을 고르시오.

1) <u>Practical</u> <u>all</u> of the Bering Sea <u>water</u> comes <u>from</u> the Pacific Ocean.
    A   B   C   D

2) <u>According</u> to many schools, sociology must <u>necessity</u> be concerned with the
    A   B
problems of justice, <u>especially</u> in matters <u>pertaining</u> to government and
                       C   D
economics.

3) The <u>discovery</u> of X—rays in 1895 <u>by W.C. Roentgen</u> <u>was</u> <u>pure</u> accidental.
      A   B   C   D

4) <u>Recent,</u> the elderly man <u>in the</u> wheelchair <u>hired</u> a young man as a <u>companion.</u>
   A   B   C   D

5) Barrett <u>had</u> to lie on his <u>left</u> side all night, and the pain <u>from</u> the wrenched
        A   B   C
shoulder became <u>some</u> worse.
              D

6) The <u>sizes</u> to atoms vary <u>regularize</u> <u>throughout</u> the periodic <u>system.</u>
     A   B   C   D

7) <u>No matter how</u> hard he is working, he will <u>insist</u> <u>on</u> the principle as <u>hardly</u> as
    A   B C   D
he can.

8) <u>The invitations</u> to <u>the dance</u> indicated that <u>everyone</u> should be dressed
       A   B   C
<u>formerly.</u>
   D

9) Influenza <u>travels</u> exactly as <u>fastly</u> as man. In <u>oxcart days</u> its progress was <u>slow.</u>
         A   B   C   D

10) The <u>following</u> night Bill returned quite <u>lately</u> from work <u>to find</u> his wife <u>lying</u>
       A   B   C   D
unconscious beside the phone.

Reading Comprehension

Questions 1-4 refer to the following letter.

Dear Ms. Fletcher,

Please accept this letter as an expression of interest in the position of Sales Manager. I have 1._____ a copy of my résumé for your review. I am familiar with the requirements for success in the sales profession, and I possess the right combination of marketing and management skills. My current 2._____ the opportunity to work in a high-pressure, team environment in which it is essential to be able to 3._____ closely with my colleagues in order to 4._____ sales deadline.

Thank you for your time and consideration.

Sincerely,
Colin Norman
Colin Norman

---

1. (A) enclosed   (B) enclose
   (C) enclosing   (D) encloses

2. (A) demanded   (B) endowed
   (C) required   (D) provided

3. (A) stress   (B) work
   (C) operate   (D) argue

4. (A) take   (B) remain
   (C) meet   (D) catch

Questions 5-7 refer to the following advertisement.

EasyFly

You can now check seat availability
and buy tickets for flights up to November 26, 2006.

To check availability, simply tel us where and when you want you want to fly. Today's flights ca be booked up to 2 hours before departure. If you're booking online with EasyFly for the first time, please read these important notes before proceeding.

---

5. What is the advertisement for?
  (A) Computers   (B) An airline
  (C) Plane tickets   (D) The Internet

6. What should the customer do first?
  (A) Read the information and access the site
  (B) Book a flight early
  (C) Tell the company which date to fly on
  (D) Read the notes

7. Why is EasyFly convenient?
  (A) Because you can buy plane tickets over the Internet
  (B) Because it's inexpensive
  (C) Because you can buy plane tickets easily
  (D) Because they have a lot of flights available

Self Review

☑ 부사에 대해 아는 대로 써보세요. 그리고 다시 한번 복습하시기 바랍니다!!!

부사의 역할과 위치	
주요 부사의 어순	
혼동되는 부사	

MEMO

VOICE

Chapter 8 VOICE

Unit 01 태의 기본형태

1. 기본 형태

I loved her. (능동태)

She was loved by me. (수동태)

2. 1, 2형식은 수동태 불가

① 1형식 동사들

go, run, fly, rise, leave for, head for

come, decline, happen, occur, rain, snow

exist, live, stand, stay

② 2형식 동사들

be, become, remain(stay)

seem/appear, prove/turn out

look, smell, taste, sound +형용사

③ 가다/오다의 느낌이 있는 단어들은 수동태 불가

arrive, appear/disappear, happen

④ 상태동사 수동태 불가

include, resemble, want, possess, have, own

Unit 02 3형식 수동태(S+V+O)

1. 기본 구조(S+V+O)

주어+be p.p by+목적격

I loved her.

= She was loved by me.

2. 주어+자동사+전치사+목적어 구조

with: deal with, agree with/on/to, interfere with, sympathize with to: object to, return to

at: laugh at, look at, arrive at

for: look for, account for

Everyone laughed at him.

= He was laughed at by everyone.

3. 주어+동사+명사절 구조

They say that he is honest.

= It is said that he is honest.

= He is said to be honest.

CheckUp 1. Select the best answer to complete each sentence.

1. The budget will (be sent, send) to the board of directors tomorrow.
2. The speaker will (awarded, be awarded) a prize after his presentation.
3. The employment contract (signed, was signed) by both the employer and the employee.
4. The banquet hall has (decorated, been decorated) for a fundraising event.
5. The manager (is considered, considers) a reliable person by the CEO.
6. These files need to be (keeping, kept) separate within each folder.
7. All the passengers (tell, are told) to get off the train.

Unit 03 4형식 수동태(S+V+IO+DO)

1. 기본 형태

① be p.p IO

② be p.p DO

③ be p.p to IO

I gave her a book.

= She was given a book by me.

= A book was given her by me.

= A book was given to her by me.

2. 3형식으로 전환 시 전치사 유의

① to: give, offer, send, bring, lend, show, tell

② for: make, buy, cook, find

③ of: ask

Unit 04 5형식 수동태(S+V+O+C)

1. 기본 구조

① 목적보어로 형/~ing/p.p

(make, keep, find)

② 목적보어로 to부정사

이때, be p.p뒤엔 to부정사가 온다.

설득류: persuade, convince, encourage, motivate, compel, force, tell, teach,

허락류: permit, allow, enable,

바람류: expect, want, would like, require

권함류: cause, remind, invite, advise, ask,

2. 특별한 5형식 동사들

① 사역동사+목적어+원형동사, p.p (let, make, have)

② get+목적어+to원형, p.p (준사역동사)

③ 지각동사+목적어+원형동사, -ing, p.p (see, hear, feel)

3. as+명사를 목적 보어로(숙어로 외울 것)

"A를 B라 간주하다"

regard A as B, look on(upon) A as B, consider A as B, take A as B,

speak of A as B, refer to A as B, cite A as B, think of A as B,

define A as B, designate A as B

4. 명사를 목적보어로 (be p.p+명사)

call, elect(be elected as B), consider A (as) B = A be considered B

appoint A (as) B = A is appointed (as) B

5. 굳어진 수동태 표현들(전치사에 유의할 것)

with: be pleased with, be satisfied with, be covered with, be crowded with

at: be disappointed at, be surprised at, be shocked at,

in: be interested in, be involved in, be absorbed in, be dressed in,

---

CheckUp 2. Select the best answer to complete each sentence.

1. Laura (bore, was born) in London.
2. State University (locates, is located) on Fifth Street.
3. A man is known (with, by) the company he keeps.
4. London is known (for, by) its fog.
5. Bill Gates is known (to, by) almost all the people in the world.
6. The suitcases were filled (by, with) Jack and his brother.
7. Was the road made (by, of) Chinese laborers?
8. What is the tower made (by, of)?
9. Wine is made (of, from) grapes.
10. Kathy is married (by, to) Paul.

Unit 05 수동태 불가 구문

① She resembles her mother.

　→*Her mother is resembled by her.

② Nobody solved this problem.

　→*This problem was solved by nobody.

　→ This problem was not solved by anybody.

③ Everyone speaks well of John.

　→*John is spoken well of.

　→ John is well spoken of.

④ He threw me a stone.

　→*I was thrown a stone by him.

　→ A stone was thrown me by him.

⑤ They robbed him of his purse.

　→*His purse was stolen from him.

　→ He was robbed of his purse by them.

⑥ I bought her a flower.

　→*She was bought a flower by me.

　→ A flower was bought (for) her by me.

⑦ They have a nice house.

  →ˑA nice house is had by them.

⑧ This dress becomes her.

  →ˑShe is become by this dress.

⑨ John hoped to kiss her.

  →ˑTo kiss her was hoped by John.

⑩ John enjoyed seeing her.

  →ˑSeeing her was enjoyed by John.

⑪ John saw himself in the mirror.

  →ˑHimself was seen in the mirror.

Unit 06 수동태 구문이 사용되는 경우

① 능동태의 주어가 분명치 않는 경우

  He was killed in the war.

② 능동태의 주어가 막연한 일반인일 경우

  English is spoken in Canada.

③ 수동태의 주어에 더 관심이 있을 경우

  The child was run over by a car.

④ 문장의 자연스런 연결을 위해

  George Foremen beat Joe Frazier, but he was beaten by Muhammad Ali.

⑤ 객관성을 부여하기 위해

  It is assumed that he will his candidacy soon.

cf. **중간태(Middle Voice)**: 능동의 형태로 수동의 의미를 갖는 경우

① This knife cuts well.

② His book sells well.

③ This pen writes well.

④ This sweater washes well.

Practice Test A

☑ 다음 빈칸에 가장 적절한 것을 고르시오.

1) Water _____ oxygen and hydrogen.
(A) consists of   (B) is consisting of
(C) is consisted of   (D) is consisted by

2) An abacus _____ for counting these days.
(A) doesn't use   (B) not used   (C) is not used   (D) is not using

3) _____ by Ms. Hopkins?
(A) Did the university found   (B) Did the university be founded
(C) Was the university found   (D) Was the university founded

4) Children _____ while they are swimming.
(A) watch   (B) must watch
(C) must be watch   (D) must be watched

5) The mentally ill _____ experts.
(A) should take care of   (B) should be take care of
(C) should be taken care of   (D) should be taken care of by

6) _____ that a Japanese oil-tanker sank near the coast yesterday.
(A) That was reported   (B) That it was reported
(C) It was reported   (D) It was reporting

7) I don't think animals in the zoo want _____ people.
(A) to look at   (B) to look at by
(C) to be looked at   (D) to be looked at by

8) The Amazon River _____ Brazil.
(A) locates   (B) is located   (C) is located by (D) is located in

9) Mr. Eastwood _____ from his job.
(A) didn't get fired   (B) got not fired
(C) not got fired   (D) got fired not

10) He is not used to _____ as a guest.
(A) treating   (B) being treated
(C) treat   (D) be treated

Practice Test B

1) All the lights in the building are _____ by the maintenance team once a month.

(A) check   (B) checking   (C) checked   (D) checks

2) This picture was _____ by a famous photographer.

(A) take   (B) taken   (C) taking   (D) took

3) All payments can _____ by credit card if the amount is over $200.

(A) make   (B) makes   (C) be make   (D) be made

4) The brochures about the new company policy _____ to the staff, both part-time and full-time workers.

(A) was distributed   (B) were distributed

(C) distributed   (D) have distributed

5) The residents _____ 30 days to move out of the building.

(A) were given   (B) gave   (C) give   (D) giving

6) The report _____ by a special committee.

(A) writes   (B) was written   (C) write   (D) are written

7) The director _____ to say that she plans to retire soon.

(A) hears   (B) heard   (C) was heard   (D) was hearing

8) I _____ to do my homework by my parents.

(A) make   (B) makes   (C) was made   (D) were made

9) The laboratory _____ with many new computers.

(A) equip   (B) equips   (C) is equipped   (D) are equipped

10) The action movie is _____ to be released in theaters next month.

(A) scheduled   (B) scheduling   (C) schedule   (D) schedules

Practice Test C

✅ 밑줄 친 부분 중 어법상 어색한 곳을 고르시오.

1) Brunei <u>is ruling</u> by a sultan <u>who</u> <u>lives</u> in a 1,700-<u>room</u> palace.
             A   B   C   D

2) <u>Bacteria</u> and viruses are <u>too small</u> <u>to see</u> by the <u>naked eyes</u>.
    A   B   C   D

3) <u>London</u> is <u>known by</u> <u>its</u> double-decker <u>buses</u>.
    A   B   C   D

4) It <u>is saying</u> that <u>a buried</u> treasure <u>was hidden</u> <u>near here</u>.
      A   B   C   D

5) <u>That is</u> believed that <u>most of</u> the earthquakes <u>occur</u> near the youngest
    A   B   C

   <u>mountain</u> ranges.
      D

6) In the future <u>many</u> space stations <u>will build</u> <u>between</u> the Earth <u>and</u> the
                 A   B   C   D

   moon.

7) Flour which <u>is made</u> <u>by grinding</u> grain <u>is used</u> to <u>making</u> bread, cake, and
               A   B   C   D

   pastry.

8) <u>Most</u> crocodiles <u>have killed</u> for their skin because <u>crocodile hides</u> make
    A   B   C

   fashionable and expensive <u>leather</u>.
                       D

9) Mrs. Williams has <u>a chance</u> of <u>electing</u> as <u>the first</u> female president <u>of her</u>
                 A   B   C

   <u>country</u>.
    D

10) About <u>a tenth of everything</u> we throw away <u>is made of</u> glass and <u>most of</u>
           A   B   C、

   it <u>can reuse</u>.
       D

Reading Comprehension

Questions 1–4 refer to the following report.

Smoking is a bad habit, and everyone knows it. The main problem, of course, is that smoking 1._____ cancer. Because of effective anti-smoking campaigns, the number of smokers in advanced countries is rapidly decreasing. But in China, very few smokers are 2._____ cigarettes. In fact, the number of teenage and female smokers continues to 3._____ every year. Many doctors say that smoking is probably one of the reasons for the high death rate of Chinese people in their 40s. After these figures were 4._____ last year, the Chinese government realized the seriousness of the problem.

1. (A) cause
   (C) can be caused
   (B) can cause
   (D) would be caused

2. (A) giving in
   (C) giving over
   (B) giving off
   (D) giving up

3. (A) increase
   (C) improve
   (B) raise
   (D) enlarge

4. (A) remembered
   (C) released
   (B) recommended
   (D) recalled

Questions 5-7 refer to the following advertisement.

Help Wanted: Customer Services Assistant

Are you highly efficient with good communication and interpersonal skill? We are a leading manufacturer of video and audio equipment and are looking for someone special with good administrative and secretarial abilities to join our very busy Customer Services Department. Salary is dependent on experience.

Apply to: Brenda Howarth, Spectro Co., 12 Pine Avenue, Detroit, IL 48130

---

5. What is the main purpose of this advertisement?
(A) To get applicants for a position which is currently vacant
(B) To apply for a job opening
(C) To inform applicants of a discount offer
(D) To encourage customers to be good servers

6. How should applicants apply for the job?
(A) By e-mail   (B) By phone
(C) By letter   (D) By fax

7. Which of the following qualities or skills is NOT mentioned?
(A) Interpersonal skills   (B) Communication skills
(C) Secretarial skills   (D) Customer service skills

Self Review

☑ 수동태에 대해 아는 대로 써보세요. 그리고 다시 한번 복습하시기 바랍니다!!!

수동태 기본형태	
3형식 수동태	
4형식 수동태	
5형식 수동태	
수동태구문이 사용되는 경우	

MEMO

INFINITIVE

Chapter 9 INFINITIVE

부정사, 동명사, 분사를 준동사라고 하는데 이는 세 품사가 모두 동사를 변환시켜 부정사는 명사, 형용사, 부사 역할을 하게하고, 동명사는 명사 역할을, 분사는 형용사 역할을 담당하게 한다. 그러므로 세 품사 모두 동사의 성질을 그대로 가지고 있으면서도 다른 기능을 하게 되는 것이 준동사의 특징이다. 특히, 동사를 가지고 만들었기 때문에 동사의 성격을 그대로 유지하고 있는 점에 유의해야 할 필요가 있다.

Unit 01 to부정사의 기본 형태와 성격

1. 기본 형태

기본형	to+동사원형	to be p.p
	to have p.p	to have been p.p
부정형	not/never to+동사원형	
원형부정사	동사원형	

2. to부정사의 의미

동사원형에 to를 붙여서 역할은 명사, 형용사, 부사로 바뀌어 사용되는 것.
그러나 동사의 성격은 유지함.

3. 부정사의 동사적 성격

① 의미상 주어를 가진다.
② 뒤에 목적어나 보어, 형식에 영향을 받음
③ 능동/ 수동의 구분
④ 시제의 구분
⑤ 수식어는 부사

CheckUp 1. Select the best answer to complete each sentence.

1. This book is good (for a child, child) to read.
2. It's dangerous (for a child, of a child) to play with matches.

3. It was impolite (for her, of her) to leave here without saying good-bye to us. I studied English hard (for me, ∅) to pass the exam.

4. It took (for me, me) two hours to clean the house.

5. It'll take nine hours (for you, you) to go to Korea from Vancouver by plane.

Unit 02 to부정사의 명사적 역할

1. 주어

① 동사가 주어자리에 오면 to부정사나 동명사로 변함

② 뒤에 목적어/보어 등이 꼭 필요

③ 주로, 가주어, 진주어 용법으로 사용

ex. It is 형용사 + (for+목적격) + to부정사

CheckUp 2. Select the best answer to complete each sentence.

1. (Make, To make) a good first impression is important.

2. It is very urgent for the company (demonstrate, to demonstrate) the quality of its products.

2. 목적어로 사용될 때

타동사 중, to부정사만을 목적어로 취하는 동사

(want, wish, hope, expect, agree, refuse, intend, decide, promise, plan)

* 자동사도 to부정사 올 때가 있다!

(fail to원형, happen to원형, seem to원형, appear to원형)

CheckUp 3. Select the best answer to complete each sentence.

1. We hope (to advertise, advertising) our new product in a weekly magazine.

2. The marketing team plans (hire, to hire) additional staff to finish the project on time.

3. 보어로 사용될 때는 주어와 일치

① 주격보어

the goal/purpose/aim/objective/plan is to원형

② 목적격보어

CheckUp 4. Select the best answer to complete each sentence.

1. The CEO wanted the employees (work, to work) on the weekend.

2. The security guard didn't allow us (enter, to enter) the building without a ticket.

Unit 03 to부정사의 형용사적 역할

명사를 수식하는 한정적 용법(항상 후치)과 보어의 역할

1. 명사 수식: 한정적 역할(미래 뜻)

① 명사 뒤 to부정사

ability, effort, way, the right, plan, means, opportunity(chance), authority

② 명사+to부정사+전치사

I have a chair to sit **on.**

He gave me some toys to play **with.**

CheckUp 5. Select the best answer to complete each sentence.

1. The factory manager is looking for the best way (to improve, improve) productivity.

2. The airline company reserves the right (refusing, to refuse) the passengers without proper identification.

2. 보어: 서술적 역할

① 주격보어: be to 용법(예정, 의무, 가능, 운명, 의도로 해석)

② 5형식의 목적보어

설득류: persuade, convince, encourage, motivate, compel, force, tell, teach

허락류: permit, allow, enable,

바람류: expect, want, would like, require

권함류: cause, remind, invite, advise, ask

CheckUp 6. Select the best answer to complete each sentence.

1. I got my friend (translate, to translate) a book for children.

2. I wanted to get this book (to translate, translated) for children.

3. Are you going to let me (eat, eating) the last piece of pizza?

4. Jane helped Kevin (finish, finishing) his homework.

5. I heard my homeroom teacher (sing, to sing) My Way.

6. The film was very sad. It made me (cry, crying).

7. Did you have the travel agent (reserve, to reserve) a hotel?

8. Kevin was made (redo, to redo) his homework by next week.

Unit 04 to부정사의 부사적 역할

1. 부사적 용법 (완전한 문장 확인 요망)

① 목적: ~하기 위해서 (to원형, in order to원형, so as to원형)

I raised my hand to ask a question.

= I raised my hand in order to ask a question.

= I raised my hand so as to ask a question.

② 감정의 원인: 해서, 하게 되어

I am sorry to hear the bad news.

③ 판단의 근거: 하다니, 하는 것을 보니

She must be a fool to believe the shocking news.

④ 결과: (했지만 결국) 하다, 되다.

He grew up to be a great scholar.

⑤ 형용사 수식

(be ready to원형, be able to원형, be likely to원형, be willing to원형, be sure/certain to원형)

He is ready to go there.

⑥ 문장 수식

To tell the truth, I don't like her.

CheckUp 7. Select the best answer to complete each sentence.

1. (Access, To access) your bank account, please enter your password.

2. The writer has to work late in order to (meeting, meet) the deadline.

3. Our company's profits are sure (increasing, to increase) due to the recent promotion.

4. The guest speaker is ready (to talk, talking) about new budget plans.

---

2. so ~ as to 구문 cf. so as to 구문과 비교

She was so sick as to go there.

= She was so sick that she couldn't go there.

CheckUp 8. Select the best answer to complete each sentence.

1. It's important (everyone, ∅) to help each other.

2. The teacher asked (for me, me) to send these letters.

Unit 05 to부정사의 문장 전환

1. too ~ to구문, enough to구문

He is too young to go to school.

= He is so young that he can't go to school.

She is old enough to go to school.

= She is so old that she can go to school.

2. 기타 to부정사의 문장 전환

① It is difficult for me to please her.

   = She is difficult for me to please.

② The snow is likely to stop soon.

   = It is likely that the snow will stop soon.

③ You are sure to succeed.

   = I am sure that you will succeed.

Unit 06 부정사와 동명사의 의미양상의 차이

부정사와 동명사의 차이

┌ **부정사**: 미래. 가설적. 미완성. 미완료. 일시적. 간접적인 현상을 표현
└ **동명사**: 과거. 실제적. 완성적. 완료. 일반적. 직접적인 현상을 표현

① I want **to go** there. (○)

   I want **going** there. (×)

② John hopes **to learn** Russian. (○)

   John hopes **learning** Russian. (×)

③ John finished **doing** his homework. (○)

   John finished **to do** his homework. (×)

④ I remember **locking** the door. (경험: 완료)

   I remember **to lock** the door. (미경험: 미완료)

⑤ I tried **closing** the window. (I closed it.)

I tried **to close** the window. (I didn't close it.)

⑥ I saw him **to enter** the room. (×)

I saw him **enter** the room. → He was seen **to enter** the room.

I saw him **entering** the room.

He made me **go** there. → I was made **to go** there by him.

⑦ He helped her **to do** her homework. (간접적 도움)

He helped her **do** her homework. (직접적 도움)

Practice Test A

1) Could you get the car _____ at once?
(A) fix   (B) fixed   (C) to fix   (D) fixing

2) This music is too hard _____.
(A) for me to correctly play   (B) for me to play correctly
(C) of me to correctly play   (D) of me to play correctly

3) What a mess! Your room needs _____.
(A) to clean   (B) to be cleaning
(C) to be cleaned   (D) to have cleaned

4) Parents are made _____ their children to school.
(A) send   (B) sent   (C) to send   (D) sending

5) Julia suggested _____ home.
(A) for us to go   (B) us to go
(C) that we should go   (D) that we went

6) My father hasn't decided _____.
(A) what is to do   (B) what does to do
(C) what to do   (D) to do what

7) It's not raining now, but it seems _____.
(A) to rain   (B) to be raining
(C) to have rained   (D) to have been rained

8) We have the store _____ the package.
(A) delive   (B) delivered   (C) to deliver   (D) delivering

9) The earth is believed _____ 4.6 billion years ago.
(A) to form   (B) to be formed
(C) to have formed   (D) to have been formed

10) They taught _____ English.
(A) speaking   (B) to speak   (C) us to speak   (D) for us to speak

Practice Test B

1) Why did you choose _____ the order?
(A) cancel   (B) cancelling   (C) to cancel   (D) cancelled

2) In an effort to _____ duplication of work, office procedures will be
   reviewed thoroughly.
(A) prevent   (B) prevented   (C) preventive   (D) preventing

3) The organizations agreed to work together _____ the financial capacity of
   small firms.
(A) improve   (B) for improve   (C) to improving (D) to improve

4) The committee chairman decided _____ on each member one by one.
(A) to call   (B) calling   (C) calls   (D) call

5) I expected my clients _____ to see me.
(A) come   (B) came   (C) coming   (D) to come

6) A sign at the entrance asked shoppers not _____ pets into the store.
(A) to bring   (B) bringing   (C) brings   (D) bring

7) We are very glad _____ with your company on the upcoming projects.
(A) work   (B) working   (C) works   (D) to work

8) It is necessary for us _____ our job on time.
(A) do   (B) to do   (C) does   (D) doing

9) It is important _____ all the computers in the office before leaving for
   the day.
(A) checking   (B) to check   (C) check   (D) checked

10) Staff are allowed _____ the laboratory facility by using a security card.
(A) access   (B) accessing   (C) to access   (D) accessible

Practice Test C

☑ 밑줄 친 부분 중 어법상 어색한 곳을 고르시오.

1) We <u>watched</u> the children <u>to playing</u> <u>soccer</u> <u>in the playground</u>.
         A   B   C   D

2) <u>At the airport</u> we can see tourists <u>come</u> and <u>to go</u> <u>all day long</u>.
   A   B   C   D

3) They had <u>the plumber</u> <u>repaired</u> the <u>broken pipe</u> <u>last week</u>.
               A   B   C   D

4) <u>It</u> was rude <u>for that man</u> <u>not to take off</u> his hat <u>in the elevator</u>.
  A   B   C   D

5) He <u>deserves</u> <u>to punish</u> <u>for</u> what <u>he did</u>.
      A   B   C   D

6) He has not <u>had</u> a job <u>for</u> a long time, so he has <u>little</u> money <u>to live</u>.
               A   B   C   D

7) Throughout <u>our lives</u> we meet many people, and <u>that</u> is important <u>to be</u>
              A   B
  <u>able to</u> judge what <u>they are</u> like.
    C   D

8) Body decoration <u>can be used</u> to make someone <u>to feel</u> and look <u>more</u>
                 A   B
  <u>attractive</u> to <u>others</u>.
    C   D

9) I <u>did</u> try <u>a lot</u>, but I found <u>that</u> almost impossible <u>to persuade</u> him to
    A   B   C   D
  change his mind.

10) <u>The fireworks</u> were <u>bright enough</u> <u>to see</u> from across <u>the lake</u>.
        A   B   C   D

Reading Comprehension

Questions 1-4 refer to the following article.

Part-time jobs are very popular with American students and usually begin during their high school days. Besides 1._____ in fast food restaurants, a very popular job for teenagers in America is baby-sitting. It is not an easy job and requires both social skills and general competence. A good baby-sitter should know how 2._____ diapers. She must be able to get the children ready for bed and keep an eye on them even while they are sleeping. Once the children are asleep, the baby-sitter is free 3._____ TV or listen to music. If she is really conscientious about her studies, she may well spend the time 4._____ homework.

1. (A) working
   (C) worked
   (B) to work
   (D) to be worked

2. (A) changing
   (C) to change
   (B) changeable
   (D) change

3. (A) watch
   (C) watching
   (B) to watch
   (D) to be watchable

4. (A) do
   (C) to do
   (B) did
   (D) doing

Questions 5-7 refer to the following letter.

Mr. Lucas Peters
523 Main Street,
Washington, DC 35291
July 15th

Dear Mr. Peters,

I am writing to confirm the arrangements for your visit to Washington next week. You will be arriving on Friday at 10 a.m. at Washington International airport and departing on Sunday at 2:30 p.m. We will send a driver to pick you up. The meeting with our lawyers will be at our office on Bond Street at 2 p.m. on Friday and should last until about 5:00 p.m.

There will be a dinner on Sunday evening, and we would be very pleased if you could attend.

Best Regards,
Linda Reed
Linda Reed

---

5. Why is Mr. Peters visiting Washington?
   (A) To have a meeting with Ms. Reed
   (B) To have a meeting with a group of lawyers
   (C) To attend the conference
   (D) To attend a special dinner in his honor

6. Why is Ms. Reed writing to Mr. Peters?
   (A) To tell him about the topic of the conference
   (B) To inform him of what will be discussed
   (C) To tell him about the dinner
   (D) To confirm the arrangements

7. How long will the meeting last?
   (A) 2 hours   (B) 2 and half hours
   (C) 3 hours   (D) 5 hours

Self Review

☑ **부정사**에 대해 아는 대로 써보세요. 그리고 다시 한번 복습하시기 바랍니다!!!

부정사의 기본형태와 성격	
부정사의 명사적 역할	
부정사의 형용사적 역할	
부정사의 부사적 역할	
부정사의 문장전환	
부정사와 동명사의 의미 차이	

10
chapter

GERUND

Chapter 10 GERUND

동명사란 동사를 주어, 목적어, 보어 즉, 명사의 자리에 쓰기 위해 명사형으로 바꾼 것이며, 명사의 성격과 동사의 성격을 같이하며 to부정사의 명사적 용법과 같다고 볼 수 있다.

Unit 01 동명사의 기본 형태와 성격

1. 동명사의 기본 형태와 성격

기본형	동사원형 + ing	being + p.p
	having + p.p	having been p.p
부정형	not/never + ing	

2. 동사의 성격

① 의미상 주어: 소유격 ~ing

② 형식에 따라 뒤에 목적어나 보어가 필요

③ 능동/ 수동태 표현 가능

④ 시제 표현 가능

⑤ 수식어–부사, 단 완전 명사화된 것은 형용사가 수식

* 부정어구: not ~ing

3. 명사와 동명사가 보기에 모두 있으면,

① 뜻의 차이가 있으면 우선은 해석이 어울리는 것

② 뜻의 차이가 거의 유사한 경우 명사를 답으로 할 것

다만, 빈칸다음에 목적어나 보어가 보이면 동사의 성격을 가지는 동명사

Unit 02 동명사의 역할 I : 주어, 목적어, 보어

1. 주어

① 뒤에 목적어나 보어 꼭 필요

② 관사나 복수형 불가능, 단수 취급

* 목적어나 보어로 인해 단/복수 혼동 유의

③ to부정사와 바꿔 쓸 수 있다.

가주어, 진주어 용법은 불가능하다.

Practicing the presentation will make you a more confident speaker.

To Practice the presentation will make you a more confident speaker.

2. 목적어

① 타동사의 목적어

The IT specialist considered installing new software.

He suggested extending the deadline by one month.

② 전치사의 목적어

Ms. Miller is used to dealing with customer complaints over the phone.

We support our product designers by having a regular meeting once a week.

3. 보어

주어와 일치해야 하고, to부정사와 바꾸어 쓸 수 있으며, 자주 쓰이지는 않음.

My favorite hobby is playing the piano.

Unit 03 동명사의 역할 Ⅱ: 동사의 목적어

1. 동명사만 목적어로 취하는 동사

mind, enjoy, give up, admit, advocate, postpone=put off, finish
avoid, suggest, consider, include, discontinue

2. to부정사만을 취하는 동사

want, hope, wish, expect, decide, plan, agree, refuse, intend, promise

3. 동명사와 to부정사 둘 다 취하면서 의미차이가 거의 없는 경우

begin, start, like, prefer, love, propose, hate, attempt, continue

4. 동명사와 to부정사 둘 다 취하면서 의미차이가 있는 경우

try, forget, remember, regret, stop

① I tried **to swim** across the river.

I tried **swimming** across the river.

② He forgot(remembered) **to lock** the door.

He forgot(remembered) **locking** the door.

③ I regret **to say** that he died in the war.

I regret **saying** that he died in the war.

④ I stopped **to smoke**.

I stopped **smoking**.

Unit 04 동명사의 역할 Ⅲ: 전치사의 목적어

1. 전치사의 목적어로 자주 쓰이는 동명사

I had difficulty (in) finding his office.

The law prohibits children from buying cigarettes.

2. to동명사 구문

I object to being treated like this.

He will be used(accustomed) to living in this city.

I am looking forward to meeting you.

When it comes to cooking, he is the best cook.

He devoted himself to studying English.

Unit 05 동명사 관용어구

① It is no use(good) crying over spilt milk.

= It is useless to cry over spilt milk.

= It is of no use to cry over spilt milk.

② There is no denying the fact.

= We can't deny the fact.

= It is impossible to deny the fact.

③ I can't help laughing at the sight.

= I can't but laugh at the sight.

= I can't choose but laugh at the sight.

= I have no choice but to laugh at the sight.

④ I feel like drinking something.

= I feel inclined to drink something.

⑤ On seeing me, he ran away.

 = As soon as he saw me, he ran away.

⑥ This is a profession of my own choosing.

 = This is a profession that I chose myself.

 = This is a profession chosen by myself.

⑦ It never rains without pouring.

 = Whenever it rains, it pours.

 = It never rains, but it pours.

⑧ He makes a point of jogging.

 = He makes it a rule to jog.

⑨ It goes without saying that man is mortal.

 = It is needless to say that man is mortal.

 = It is matter of course to say that man is mortal.

⑩ She was far from being satisfied.

 = She was never being satisfied.

⑪ What do you say to having a break?

 = What about having a break?

⑫ The moon was on the point of rising.

 = The moon was about to rise.

⑬ Instead of being shy, she is unsocial.

 = She is not shy, but unsocial.

CheckUp 1. Select the best answer to complete each sentence.

1. Ms. Williams has a chance of (be electing, being elected) as the first female president in her country.

2. I feel sorry about (writing not, not writing) to you sooner.

3. Reading a lot of books (is, are) important for children.

4. Jogging and swimming (is, are) my favorite activities.

5. Did you enjoy (being, to be) with your family on vacation last summer?

6. It's better to avoid (traveling, to travel) during rush hour.

7. The doctor suggested (taking, to take) a rest as often as possible.

8. You need (to repair, repairing) the car.

9. The car needs (to repair, repairing).

10. Are you looking forward to (visit, visiting) Egypt?

Practice Test A

☑ 다음 빈칸에 가장 적절한 것을 고르시오.

1) Kevin was scolded for _____ on time.
(A) not to come   (B) to not come   (C) not coming   (D) coming not

2) _____ tends to weaken as we grow old.
(A) We hearing   (B) We to hear   (C) Our hearing   (D) Our to hear

3) He was awakened _____.
(A) by the dog bark   (B) by the dog to bark
(C) by the dog's to bark   (D) by the dog's barking

4) We appreciate _____ our friends last night.
(A) you help   (B) you to help   (C) your to help   (D) your helping

5) We regret _____ you he died as a consequence of his injuries.
(A) inform   (B) informing   (C) to inform   (D) to have informed

6) I can't remember _____ to the hospital after I fell down in the classroom.
(A) to take   (B) to be taken   (C) taking   (D) being taken

7) I need another VCR _____ videotapes.
(A) for copy   (B) to copy   (C) for copying   (D) to copying

8) Did you have _____ my office?
(A) difficulty finding   (B) difficulty to find
(C) difficulties finding   (D) difficulties to find

9) An old man walking along the road stopped _____ to us.
(A) talk   (B) to talk   (C) talking   (D) being talked

10) What can you do to keep it _____ again?
(A) to happen   (B) happening
(C) from happening   (D) about happening

Practice Test B

1) She doesn't like _____ in front of people.
(A) speak   (B) speaking   (C) speaks   (D) spoke

2) The country needs a big _____ in education.
(A) invest   (B) investing   (C) to invest   (D) investment

3) We will _____ spending more money on the facility.
(A) offer   (B) postpone   (C) make   (D) expect

4) Mr. Tanaka is devoted to _____ for old people in need.
(A) care   (B) cared   (C) caring   (D) being cared

5) Our chef insists on _____ organic ingredients in his dishes.
(A) use   (B) to use   (C) using   (D) uses

6) The rain continued _____ all afternoon.
(A) fall   (B) falling   (C) fallen   (D) fell

7) I am used to _____ in an apartment, but now he doesn't.
(A) live   (B) to live   (C) living   (D) lived

8) Mike used to _____ glasses, but now he doesn't.
(A) wear   (B) to wear   (C) wearing   (D) weared

9) Flour is used _____ bread and noodles.
(A) make   (B) to make   (C) making   (D) made

10) You must remember _____ your uncle at 3 o'clock. It's important.
(A) call   (B) to call   (C) calling   (D) called

Practice Test C

☑ 밑줄 친 부분 중 어법상 어색한 곳을 고르시오.

1) <u>To speaking</u> English <u>is</u> <u>even</u> more difficult than <u>reading</u> it.
      A   B   C   D

2) <u>Working</u> for <u>poor people</u> <u>are</u> <u>much important</u> in the modern societies than
     A   B   C   D
  before.

3) <u>In the music industry</u> record companies <u>are responsible for</u> everything from
            A   B
  <u>to develop</u> new talent <u>to</u> promoting CDs.
     C   D

4) Although <u>it</u> rained so <u>heavily</u>, the runners just kept <u>from</u> <u>running</u>.
           A   B   C   D

5) We have <u>decided to</u> stop <u>to interview</u> applicants <u>who are</u> willing to work <u>as</u>
           A   B   C
  <u>volunteers</u>.
     D

6) <u>No one</u> will <u>be allowed to</u> enter <u>the meeting place</u> without <u>inviting</u>.
    A   B   C   D

7) The doctor said <u>that</u> <u>further</u> treatment <u>would</u> prevent cancer <u>to develop</u>.
               A   B   C   D

8) <u>Eating</u> of a well-prepared meal <u>is considered</u> one of the important <u>pleasures</u>
   A   B   C
  of <u>daily</u> life.
      D

9) <u>The doctor</u> we met yesterday <u>insisted on</u> <u>we</u> moving to a <u>milder</u> climate.
    A   B   C   D

10) Please remember <u>enclosing</u> <u>a</u> stamped <u>addressed</u> envelope when <u>writing</u>.
                A   B   C   D

Reading Comprehension

Questions 1–4 refer to the following news report.

Americans have long had an international reputation for 1._____ in love with their guns. Two hundred years ago, when the U.S. constitution was written, it was necessary 2._____ a gun for hunting. According to recent polls, however, a majority of voters are now in favor of Congress's passing more laws 3._____ handguns. People around the world think the American gun culture is crazy. At this time, banning guns completely is a good idea. Americans must stop 4._____ of themselves as people who need weapons to survive.

1. (A) being
   (C) to have been
   (B) to be
   (D) be

2. (A) owning
   (C) to own
   (B) own
   (D) to have owned

3. (A) control
   (C) controllable
   (B) controlled
   (D) to control

4. (A) think
   (C) to think
   (B) thinking
   (D) thinkable

Questions 5-7 refer to the following letter.

Mr. Tom Schmidt
910 Hill Street,
Chicago, IL 35291

Dear Mr. Schmidt,

I am the marketing manager for Valdez, a small Spanish pharmaceutical company. We met briefly at the conference in New York last November.

In your presentation in New York, you mentioned that your company was interested in entering the Spanish market. We have had many years of experience and believe that we are in a strong position to be local partner for your company in Spain. I am coming to Germany next month and wondered whether you would be interested in meeting to discuss this further. Could you let me know by the end of the week?

I am including some information about our company. If you need any further information, please do not hesitate to contact me. I look forward to hearing from you.

Sincerely yours,
Fernando Montenegro
Fernando Montenegro

---

5. Who is Fernando Montenegro working for?

   (A) A marketing company with many years of experience
   (B) A drug manufacturing company in Spain
   (C) An advertising company in Spain
   (D) A local company in Germany

6. Why does Fernando Montenegro want to meet Mr. Schmidt?

   (A) To become a partner company
   (B) To want his presentation in New York
   (C) To let him know about business in Spain
   (D) To discuss legal issues regarding doing business in Spain

7. Why does Fernando Montenegro think his company would be a good business partner?

    (A) Because he has already met Mr. Schmidt

    (B) Because he liked Mr. Schmidt's presentation

    (C) Because his company held the conference in New York

    (D) Because his company has many years of experience in Spain

Self Review

☑ **동명사**에 대해 아는 대로 써보세요. 그리고 다시 한번 복습하시기 바랍니다!!!

동명사의 기본 형태와 성격	
동명사만을 목적어로 취하는 동사	
부정사만을 목적어로 취하는 동사	
둘 다 취하는 동사	
동명사 관용어구	

MEMO

11

chapter

PARTICIPLE

Chapter 11 PARTICIPLE

Unit 01 분사의 기본 형태와 의미

1. 의미와 기본 형태

① 분사란 동사가 형용사가 된 것

② 역할: 형용사 역할로 명사를 수식하거나 보어로 쓰임

③ 종류: 현재분사, 과거 분사

④ 차이: 현재분사 - 능동, 진행

　　　　과거분사 - 수동, 완료

⑤ 1) 순수 형용사 Vs. 분사: 형용사 우선의 법칙

　　2) 상태가 아닌 동사적 성격이 강한 경우 분사 사용

현재분사	동사원형+ing	being p.p	능동, 진행
과거분사	동사원형+(e)d 불규칙	having been p.p	수동, 완료

2. 현재분사(능동, 진행)

① 한정적 용법

A rolling stone gathers no moss.

People visiting the place are increasing.

CheckUp 1. Select the best answer to complete each sentence.

1. People (applying, applied) for the position should submit a résumé.
2. The candidates were asked some (confusing, confused) questions during their interviews.
3. The hotel is offering (reducing, reduced) rates on deluxe rooms this month.
4. The ideas (suggesting, suggested) by Ms. Rose were very innovative.

---

② 서술적 용법

She stood looking at the picture.

I saw her entering the room.

CheckUp 2. Select the best answer to complete each sentence.

1. The public's response to the new product was (disappointing, disappointed).
2. The company is (pleased, pleasing) to announce that Ms. Gibson has been appointed sales manager.
3. I talk a lot with my clients to help them get (satisfying, satisfied) results.

3. 과거분사(수동, 완료)

① 한정적 용법

The revised law will take effect soon.

The fallen leaves were scattered all over the place.

For a limited time only, you can purchase this item at a reduced price.

② 서술적 용법

He is concerned about your waste of time.

I had the car repaired by him.

CheckUp 3. Select the best answer to complete each sentence.

1. A (barking, barked) dog never bites.
2. A (closed, closing) mind is a dying mind.
3. China is a (developing, developed) country.
4. America is the (developing, developed) country.
5. My mother was (surprising, surprised) at my result on the final exam.
6. The news was so (surprising, surprised).
7. Mark is a (good-looking, looking-good) boy.
8. It is (newly-built, built-newly) library.
9. Nylon is an (man-made, man-making) material.
10. That is an (eye-catching, eye-caught) building.

Unit 02 분사의 위치

① 명사의 바로 앞/뒤
② be -ing/p.p (2형식)
③ 5형식의 목적보어 자리 (5형식)

Unit 03 현재분사로만 쓰이는 경우

a lasting impression, missing luggage, misleading information, opening hours, an existing facility, preceding years, incoming calls, an opposing point of view, disappointing revenue, approaching storm, rewarding discussion, encouraging remark, challenging tasks, demanding customers

Unit 04 과거분사로만 쓰이는 경우

complicated problems, preferred methods, dedicated employees, experienced employees, motivated employees, qualified applicants, distinguished scholars, informed decision, detailed information, attached resume, involved tasks

---

CheckUp 4. Select the best answer to complete each sentence.

1. The fact became (known, knowing) all over the world.
2. She heard her name (calling, called, call).
3. He walked about the room with his arms (folding, folded)
4. I found my friend (working, worked) at his desk.
5. She was a girl (named, naming) Jane Smith.
6. I must have my decayed teeth (pull, pulled) out.
7. He lies (burying, buried) in that churchyard.
8. A (drowned, drowning) man will catch at a straw.
9. I cannot make myself (understand, understood) in English.
10. Of those (invited, inviting) only two came to the party.

Unit 05 알아두면 좋은 분사구조

① before/ after + ~ing
② 주어+ 동사 ...., ~ing
③ 명사 ~ing 명사
④ 감정동사들(excite, interest, embarrass, disappoint, bor e등)
    ⓐ 그 감정을 느끼면 p.p, 그 감정을 주면 ~ing
    ⓑ 주로 사람이면 p.p, 사물이면 ~ing를 많이 사용

(감정을 주면) 현재분사		(감정을 느끼면) 과거분사	
satisfying	만족시키는	satisfied	만족한
embarrassing	당황하게 하는	embarrassed	당황한
pleasing	즐겁게 하는	pleased	즐거운
frustrating	좌절시키는	frustrated	좌절한
amazing	놀라게 하는	amazed	놀란
frightening	무섭게 하는	frightened	무서운
disappointing	실망하게 하는	disappointed	실망한
annoying	짜증나게 하는	annoyed	짜증이 난
touching	감동을 주는	touched	감동한
relieving	안도하게 하는	relieved	안도한

Unit 06 분사구문

부사절(복문이나 중문)이 분사구문을 통해서 단문이 됨

1. 분사구문으로 전환하는 방법

① 접속사는 없앰. cf. 뜻을 분명히 하기 위해 접속사를 살려둘 때도 있음

② 복문일 때 → 부사절을 분사구문으로

③ 중문일 때 → 시제가 높은 쪽을 분사구문으로
　　　　　　　시제가 같은 쪽은 부사적 의미로
　　　　　　　바꿀 수 있는 부분을 분사구문으로

④ 주어(같을 때 없앤다, 다를 때는 그대로)

⑤ 동사는 능동은 -ing로 수동일 때는 -p.p로
　　　　　　완료수동일 때는 -p.p나 having been p.p로
　　　　　　진행일 때는 -ing로 바꿈

2. 부사절로 고칠 때의 접속사

① 시간: when, while, after, before, as 등
When I was walking along the street, I met an old friend of mine.
→ Walking along the street, I met an old friend of mine.

② 원인(이유): as, since, because 등
As he lives in a remote village, he has few visitors.
→ Living in a remote village, he has few visitors.

③ 조건: if, unless(=if~not) 등

If you turn to the left, you will see the station.

→ Turning to the left, you will see the station.

④ 양보: though, although 등

Though I admit what you say, I still think you are wrong.

→ Admitting what you say, I still think you are wrong.

⑤ 부대상황: as= and- (하자면, 그리고, 또-)

Father watched television, and he drank a glass of wine.

→ Father watched television, drinking a glass of wine.

CheckUp 5. Select the best answer to complete each sentence.

1. (Researching, Researched) the firm carefully, Susan decided to buy the stock.

2. (Browsing, Browsed) the store for a couple of hours, she finally decided to buy a pair of gloves for her colleague's birthday.

---

3. 분사구문의 시제

① 단순분사(동원+-ing/ being pp): 주절과 종속절이 동일 시제

② 완료분사(having pp/ having been pp): 주절보다 종속절이 하나 앞선 시제.

   ⓐ Because I have no money with me, I cannot buy the car.

     = Having no money with me, I cannot buy the car.

   ⓑ After she had finished her shopping, she went home.

     = Having finished her shopping, she went home.

4. 분사구문의 의미상 주어

① 일반형 분사구문: 분사구문의 S.S와 주절의 주어가 같을 때는 반드시 생략

② 독립 분사구문: 분사구문의 S.S와 주절의 주어가 다를 때는 반드시 기록

   ⓐ When I was walking in the park, I met him.

     = Walking in the park, I met him.

   ⓑ After the sun had set in the west, we started.

     = The sun having set in the west, we started.

CheckUp 6. 다음 문장의 구는 절로, 절은 분사구문으로 바꿀 때 빈칸에 적절한 단어를 쓰시오.

1. Taken by surprise, he gave up the contest.

   = As he (   ) (   ) by surprise, he gave up the contest.

2. His work done, he sat down to rest for a moment.

   = After his work (   ) (   ) done, he sat down to rest for a moment.

3. It being Sunday, the park was crowded with children.

   = (   ) it was Sunday, the park was crowded with children.

4. Supper ready, we went into the dinning room.

   = As supper (   ) ready, we went into the dinning room.

5. As there was nothing to do, he was allowed to go home.

   = There (   ) nothing to do, he was allowed to go home.

6. If we consider his age, his conduct should not be blamed.

   = (   ) his age, his conduct should not be blamed.

7. As the weather did not improve, the plan had to be changed.

   = The weather (   ) improving, the plan had to be changed.

8. After I had finished my task, I took a walk.

   = (   ) finished my task, I took a walk.

9. If we judge from his accent, he seems to be an American.

   = (   ) from his accent, he seems to be an American.

10. If you turn to the right, you will find the department store on your left.

   = (   ) to the right, you will find the department store on your left.

Unit 07 유의해야 할 분사 구문

1. 의미상 주어

   ① As he is honest, everyone loves him.

      = Being honest, he is loved by everyone.

      (분사의 의미상 주어에 I, you, He, She, We, They 등과 같은 인칭대명사 주어를 따로 명시하지 않는 것이 바람직함.)

   ② As my mother is sick, I can't go out.

      = My mother being sick, I can't go out.

2. 부대상황의 부사구

   "with+ 목적어 + 여러 요소"(현재분사, 과거분사, 부사구, 형용사)

   ① He went out with his dog following.

   ② He was sitting on the beach with his legs crossed.

   ③ Don't speak with your mouth full.

   ④ He was taking a leisurely walk with a pipe in his mouth.

3. 분사구문의 의미상 주어와 주절의 주어 일치

① Having read the book, it was thrown away.(?)

   → Having read the book, I threw it away.

② Being Sunday, I went to church.(?)

   → It being Sunday, I went to church.

4. 의사분사: "명사+ing, pp" "-을(를) 가진"으로 해석

① a blue-eyed girl(=a girl with blue eyes)

② a three-legged stool(=a stool with three legs)

5. (분사구문의 강조)

  ┌ 현재분사 강조: as+ 주어+ do동사
  └ 과거분사 강조: as+ 주어+ be동사

① Living as I do in a remote village, I have few visitors.

② Hidden as it was by the curtain, I could not find it.

6. 동명사와 분사의 차이

① 현재분사 + 명사

a sleeping baby =a baby who is sleeping

boiling water =water which is boiling

the following example =the example which follows

② 동명사 + 명사

a sleeping car =a car used or intended for sleeping

a living room =a room where one lives when not sleeping

a smoking room =a room for smoking

7. 분사형 전치사

considering: ~에 비해서, ~을 고려하면

notwithstanding: ~에도 불구하고

excepting: ~을 제외하고

touching: ~에 관해서

regarding: ~에 관해서

8. 무인칭 독립분사구문

분사구문의 의미상 주어와 주절의 주어가 다를 때는 의미상 주어를 반드시 밝혀 주어야
하나 일반인이 주어일 때는 관용적으로 생략

① If(When) we judge from the rumor, he seems to be dishonest.

   = Judging from the rumor, he seems to be dishonest.

② If we speak generally =Generally speaking,

   If we speak strictly =Strictly speaking,

   If we speak properly =Properly speaking,

   If we speak correctly =Correctly speaking,

   If we speak roughly =Roughly speaking,

   If we speak frankly =Frankly speaking,

   If we talk of movies, I don't like sad movies.

   = Talking of movies, I don't like sad movies.

   If we judge from what people say, he must be a great scholar.

   = Judging from what people say, he must be a great scholar.

   If we take all things into consideration,

   = Taking all things into consideration,

   Granting that you were drunk, you are responsible for the accident.

   Seeing that he is still young, he will recover soon.

   Considering(For) his age, he is very tall.

Practice Test A

☑ 다음 빈칸에 가장 적절한 것을 고르시오.

1) He spoke for a long time and his speech was very _____.
(A) boring   (B) bored   (C) bore   (D) boredom

2) _____ the work, I went to the movies.
(A) Finishing   (B) Being finished
(C) Finished   (D) Having finished

3) An expensive book _____ to this club is lost.
(A) belong   (B) belongs   (C) belonging   (D) was belonging

4) The first commercial film _____ in California was completed in 1907.
(A) made   (B) was made   (C) to make   (D) making

5) I thought I saw professor Davis _____ in the library last night.
(A) working   (B) worked   (C) to work   (D) works

6) I am sorry, but there isn't _____.
(A) any left   (B) leaving any   (C) left any   (D) some left

7) _____ in all parts of the state, pines are the most common tree in Georgia.
(A) Found   (B) Finding them
(C) To find them   (D) They are found

8) _____ built, with poor vision but excellent senses of smell and hearing, the bear will eat almost anything
(A) It is heavily   (B) Heavily
(C) That it is heavily   (D) When is it heavily

9) He had his temperature _____ in the hospital.
(A) taking   (B) taken   (C) to take   (D) take

10) Please provide your _____ time of arrival when you reply.
(A) estimate   (B) estimating   (C) estimated   (D) estimation

Practice Test B

1) If we practice proper maintenance of _____ equipment, we don't need to make new purchases so frequently.
(A) exists   (B) to exist   (C) existing   (D) existed

2) Websites _____ by professionals look better and are easier to use.
(A) design   (B) designing   (C) to design   (D) designed

3) The name and address of the person _____ the conference are enclosed in this e-mail.
(A) organized   (B) organization   (C) has organized (D) organizing

4) A _____ schedule was sent to the company prior to production.
(A) detailing   (B) detailed   (C) details   (D) in detail

5) Anyone _____ in our services can visit our office and get additional information.
(A) interest   (B) interesting   (C) interested   (D) interests

6) _____ to take a day off, Kevin went to see a doctor for a medical check-up.
(A) Allow   (B) Allowing   (C) To allow   (D) Allowed

7) The man _____ the piano on the stage is my brother.
(A) to play   (B) playing   (C) played   (D) play

8) _____ down the street, I ran into my old friend.
(A) Walk   (B) Walking   (C) To walk   (D) Walked

9) Most of the executives were _____ with last quater's sales figures.
(A) disappoint   (B) disappointed
(C) disappointment   (D) disappointing

10) There are many books in the library _____ the history of Korea.
(A) describe   (B) described   (C) describing   (D) description

Practice Test C

✅ 밑줄 친 부분 중 어법상 어색한 곳을 고르시오.

1) <u>Shocking</u> at the news, his father <u>said</u> <u>nothing</u> and <u>fell</u> down.
    A   B   C   D

2) <u>Scientists</u> still <u>can't find</u> any <u>convinced</u> link between <u>intelligence and the</u>
   A   B   C   D
<u>quantity</u> or quality of brain cells.

3) <u>Romanticists</u> <u>show life as being</u> more <u>emotionally excited and satisfying</u> than it
      A   B   C
<u>normally</u> is.
  D

4) He also told of <u>frightened</u> events that had <u>taken place</u> in his native state of
               A   B
Connecticut and <u>listed</u> the <u>fearful</u> things he has seen on his nightly walks in
                C   D
Sleepy hollow.

5) We can supplement our town ideas <u>with</u> information and <u>data</u> <u>gathering</u> from
                            A   B   C
our reading, our observation, <u>and so forth</u>.
                            D

6) Louisa may Alcott is chiefly <u>remembered</u> for little Women, <u>one</u> of the most
                         A   B
<u>popular</u> girl's books ever <u>wrote</u>.
  C   D

7) Beverly Hills, a residential community <u>surrounding</u> by the city of Los Angeles is
                                 A
<u>famous</u> for its <u>luxurious</u> homes and many exclusive <u>shops</u>.
  B   C   D

8) Dorothea Dix, <u>was known</u> for her work <u>to improve</u> mental institutions, <u>served</u>
              A   B   C
as superintendent of <u>nurses</u> during the American Civil War.
                 D

9) <u>Those</u> <u>interesting</u> in <u>signing</u> up for the class <u>should</u> do so immediately.
  A   B   C   D

10) <u>The loser team</u> protested that <u>they</u> had not been given <u>impartial treatment</u> <u>by</u>
      A   B   C   D
the officials.

Reading Comprehension

Questions 1-4 refer to the following the article.

As Americans moved from the center of towns into the suburbs, a new style of shopping 1._____, and malls, which reflected the new lifestyles of modern living, began to spring up everywhere. Most Americans today prefer to shop at such malls because of their convenience and accessibility. 2._____ by huge parking lots, the many shops and stores offer a wide variety of goods at a wide range of prices. Within every mall, there are even banks 3._____ a full supply of services for the consumer. Activities 4._____ for all members of the family.

1. (A) needs
   (C) to be needed
   (B) was needed
   (D) is need

2. (A) Flanked
   (C) To flank
   (B) Flanking
   (D) To be flanked

3. (A) which are offered
   (C) which offer
   (B) that offers
   (D) that have been offered

4. (A) provide
   (C) to provide
   (B) are providing
   (D) are provided

Come to Kauai & Vacation
Hawaiian Style

Horseback ride on the beach — Eat Kona lobster
Bicycle down a mountain — Watch hula dancers
Snorkel — Stay at the Hyatt Regency
Take a helicopter ride — Relax and swim in the pool

Contact Tricia Pensky at Paradise Travel: pensky@goodearth.com or call
643-9988

To: pensky@goodearth.com
From: sheridan@acrobat.org

Dear Ms. Pensky,

My Family and I are really interested in vacationing in Hawaii this winter.
I saw your ad in the paper, but noticed there isn't much information
regarding prices and dates, so I hope you can answer a few questions.
First, what would the price be for a package for two adults and two
children leaving December 27th and returning January 10th. Also, the
Hyatt may be a little pricey. Are there options for staying at other hotels?
Finally, I'm an avid golfer and would like you to send me some
information regarding golf packages.

Sincerely,

Peter Sheridan

---

5. What information is NOT in th ad?
   (A) Information about accommodation
   (B) Information about recreation activities
   (C) Information about golf packages
   (D) Information about available food choices

6. What activity is NOT mentioned in the ad?

   (A) Bicycling down a mountain

   (B) Relaxing and swimming in the pool

   (C) Taking a helicopter ride

   (D) Exploring caves

7. How many people are included in the vacation package Peter asks about?

   (A) Two adults and three children

   (B) Two adults only

   (C) Two families

   (D) Two adults and two children

8. The word "pricey" in passage 2, line 5 is closest in meaning to?

   (A) Expensive   (B) Near the beach

   (C) Cheap   (D) Comfortable

9. What would Peter like Tricia to send him information about?

   (A) Touring the island   (B) Golf packages

   (C) Going surfing   (D) The best beaches for swimming

Self Review

분사에 대해 아는 대로 써보세요. 그리고 다시 한번 복습하시기 바랍니다!!!

기본 형태와 의미	
분사의 위치	
현재분사로 쓰이는 경우	
과거분사로 쓰이는 경우	
분사구문	

MEMO

12 chapter

PREPOSITION

Chapter 12 PREPOSITION

Unit 01 전치사의 기본 이해

1. 구조와 역할

① 구조는 뒤에 나오는 명사와 결합해서 전명구를 이룸

　1) 전치사 + 일반 명사 (on the internet)

　2) 전치사 + 대명사 목적격 (between you and me)

　3) 전치사 + 동명사 (by-ing, without -ing)

　4) 전치사 + 전명구 (from around the world, except in the room)

② 역할은 형용사나 부사 역할을 함

CheckUp 1. Select the best answer to complete each sentence.

1. These days, employees can do their work without (leave, leaving) home.
2. Feel free to leave your luggage with (we, us) while you're away.
3. If you find the products defective, you should return them (by, to) next Saturday.
4. Admission to the Ubud Hanging Garden is free every Monday from 2:00 p.m. to 4:00 p.m. (without, throughout) the summer.

---

2. 다양한 의미의 전치사

① ~분야에서 증가, 감소(in): in the sales department, advances in, experience in, be busy in ~ing, have difficulty in ~ing,

② ~아래/~중(under): under management, ~supervision, control, construction, development, consideration

③ ~로서(as): as a teacher

④ ~로, ~없이(with/without): without having to, without exceptions, with a balance of, with the aim of, problem with

⑤ ~을 통해서(through): through the use of, through arbitration

⑥ ~함으로써(by): by ~ing, by 숫자: ~만큼

⑦ 속도 등(at): at: 속도, 가격, 주소, 번호, 홈페이지

⑧ 용도나 대상(for): 용도, 대상: for sale, for visitors

⑨ 계속(on): on the rise/the wane, on one's way to

⑩ 넘어선, 밖에(beyond): beyond expectation, beyond control

⑪ ~에 관한(over): concern over, dispute over

⑫ ~에 대한(on, about): information on/ about

3. 명사 of 명사 구조

① 주격: a recent outbreak of Corona 19

② 소유격: the leg of this desk

③ 목적격: the development of this city

④ 동격: the aim of fulfilling his job

4. 양보의 전치사(despite, in spite of, with all, for all)

5. 이유의 전치사(because of, due to, owing to, on account of, thanks to)

CheckUp 2. Select the best answer to complete each sentence.

1. (Due to, During) the high salary, a lot of potential employees submitted application forms on the first day.

2. (Thanks to, Instead of) your hard work, our company was chosen for the award.

Unit 02 시점 vs. 기간의 전치사

① by Vs. until "~할 때 까지" (시점)
 : by는 일회적/단발성 동작 일 때(submit, return, receive, inform 등)
   until은 지속적 일 때(stay, wait, continue, remain, last 등)

② for Vs. during "~하는 동안" (기간)
 : for+숫자, during+기간명사

③ throughout Vs. over (기간)
 : throughout (처음부터 끝까지 계속) −throughout the conference
   over(어떤 기간에 걸쳐서 쭉 계속) −over the past three years
    * over대신, in, for등도 가능

④ within Vs. in
 : within ~ 이내에(능력, 기간, 범위)
   in+시간: ~시간 후에, in+물리적 장소

    * within +기간, by+시점

⑤ before=prior to, after=following

Unit 03 시간의 전치사

① at+정확시각

② on+요일, 날짜

③ in+오전, 오후, 저녁, 달, 계절, 세기

④ 다음은 전치사(in, on) 안 씀 −부사로 쓰이기 때문

    (last~, this~, next~, yesterday, today, tomorrow, tonight)

Unit 04 장소의 전치사

① 장소 전치사

    at, in, on, over, under, above, below, beside, between/among, behind,

② 장소 전치사

    for/toward, to, into, out of, from, through, around/round, along,

    cross/across, beyond/within, up/down, over/under,

CheckUp 3. Select the best answer to complete each sentence.

1. The marketing team is (on, against) the fifth floor.

2. Guests are asked to leave their keys (in, over) the box on the c

3. Trees have been planted (along, above) the streets.

4. The general manager went (out of, through) the office to have a meeting
   with important clients.

Unit 05 그 외 주요 전치사

1. ~을 제외하고

① except(직설법, 현재 있는 것) ~을 제외하고(문장 맨 앞에는 잘 쓰지 않음)

    except=but=except for=excepting 모두 전치사임

    except that(when)+S+V, S+V

② barring(가정법, 미래에 있을 것) ~을 제외 한다면(=but for=without)

③ excluding+명사, including ～을 포함하여

CheckUp 4. Select the best answer to complete each sentence.

1. You can come to the office to ask questions anytime (except, about) on Thursday.
2. The store has to stay open, (notwithstanding, except for) our staffing problems.
3. (Considering, Including) the circumstances, we have to give up the project as of today.
4. Our company sometimes sends an e-mail (including, excluding) a special offer coupon to increase sales.

---

2. 기타 전치사

① ～에 관하여: concerning, regarding, about, as to/ as for, with(in) regard(respect, reference) to

② by+교통, 통신 수단

③ ～외에도: besides, in addition to, apart from, aside from on top of, as well as

④ besides, moreover, in addition, as well은 부사도 가능

CheckUp 5. Select the best answer to complete each sentence.

1. The tiger is (in, into) the cage.
2. Vicky is diving (in, into) the water.
3. Rachel is waiting for me (at, on) the bus stop.
4. There are twelve bridges (on, over) Han River.
5. Jessica is sitting (next to, near to) Emma.
6. Who is the last person waiting (in, on) the line?
7. I've been working (since, for) eight hours without stopping.
8. The car accident happened (during, at) the night.
9. I have to finish this report (by, till) Tuesday.
10. How long does it take from here to Beijing (by, in) plane?

Practice Test A

✅ 밑줄 친 어법상 가장 적절한 것을 고르시오.

1) Are you going to Busan, _____ plane or _____ your car?
(A) by-by   (B) by-in   (C) in-by   (D) in-in

2) Mr. Frodesen has worked as a journalist _____ ten years _____ 1992.
(A) for-since   (B) since-for   (C) for-from   (D) since-from

3) Jane is an aerobic instructor, but she plays the flute _____ an expert.
(A) like   (B) since   (C) as   (D) as if

4) The police prevented the crime from _____.
(A) take place   (B) took place   (C) taking place   (D) to take place

5) In spite of _____, I could not sleep.
(A) I was tired   (B) that I was tired
(C) the fact I was tired   (D) the fact that much wind

6) It was cold, dark, and _____.
(A) windy   (B) with wind
(C) it was windy   (D) there was much wind

7) Grammar is needed to both speak _____ English.
(A) and write   (B) and to write
(C) also write   (D) also to write

8) Vicky like both gardening _____ to music.
(A) also listening   (B) also to listen
(C) and listening   (D) and to listen

9) Neither Jane nor her parents _____ present at the meeting.
(A) was   (B) were   (C) was not   (D) were not

10) You should get the license right now. _____, you'll have to pay a fine.
(A) However   (B) Otherwise   (C) Therefore   (D) Moreover

Practice Test B

1) Please register in _____, and you will get a 5% discount.

(A) advance   (B) advances   (C) advancing   (D) advanced

2) High-Quality Health Care & Restoration has been providing excellent services _____ over twenty years.

(A) among   (B) with   (C) for   (D) since

3) According to a recent study, smoking rates have been increasing _____ women.

(A) between   (B) among   (C) on   (D) with

4) Only people with ID cards can pass _____ the main gate.

(A) to   (B) among   (C) below   (D) through

5) You can increase your energy _____ taking a short nap.

(A) at   (B) by   (C) for   (D) with

6) You will be amazed _____ the speed and power of this new laptop.

(A) at   (B) from   (C) for   (D) with

7) _____ event coordinator, Ms. Parker is supposed to select a venue for the workshop.

(A) Of   (B) As   (C) About   (D) On

8) Management responded favorably to the prospective employees' concerns _____ the benefits package.

(A) regard   (B) regards   (C) regarded   (D) regarding

9) Customers are satisfied with the products _____ the high price.

(A) because of   (B) besides   (C) instead of   (D) despite

10) I like this government. I especially am _____ their economic policies.

(A) for   (B) against   (C) to   (D) by

Practice Test C

☑ 밑줄 친 부분 중 어법상 어색한 곳을 고르시오.

1) <u>Most of</u> the publishing companies are busiest <u>on December</u> <u>because</u> they
     A   B   C

  have to print and plan new books for <u>the next year</u>.
                                      D

2) <u>Alike</u> Earth, Mars <u>has</u> polar ice caps at <u>its</u> northern and southern <u>poles</u>.
    A   B   C   D

3) The <u>fire-fighters</u> stopped <u>the fire</u> <u>from</u> <u>to spread</u>.
           A   B   C   D

4) Rachel <u>is tired of</u> <u>that she</u> always has to work <u>on</u> <u>Sundays</u>.
           A   B   C   D

5) My father is <u>a very active</u> person; he likes <u>to ski</u>, to climb mountains and
                 A   B

  <u>fishing</u> in <u>the sea</u>.
    C   D

6) <u>Even though</u> he is young, he <u>does</u> his work <u>quickly</u>, carefully, and <u>with ease</u>.
      A   B   C   D

7) We <u>got up</u> early, <u>ate</u> breakfast, and <u>the house was cleaned</u>—all <u>before</u> my
       A   B   C   D

  aunt arrived.

8) Penny <u>always</u> loved growing <u>flowers</u> and <u>to walk</u> through <u>the park</u>.
           A   B   C   D

9) Kevin's father gave him <u>some good advice</u>. He, <u>otherwise</u>, did not follow <u>it</u>.
                         A   B   C   D

10) Not only you <u>but also</u> Jennifer <u>are going</u> to <u>get a scholarship</u> to <u>Yonsei</u>
                  A   B   C

  <u>University</u>.
    D

Reading Comprehension

Questions 1-4 refer to the following notice.

You are notified that you owe the 1._____ landlord the sum of $780.00, being rent for the premises 2._____ in the City of Wellington, Illinois. You are further notified that payment of the sum is overdue and is demanded of you, and that unless payment 3._____ on or before June 24, 2006, your possession of the premises 4._____. Only full payment of the rent demanded in this notice, within five days of the date on which you are served this notice, will cancel the landlord's right to end the lease.

1. (A) undersigned   (B) undersigning
   (C) undersign   (D) be undersigned

2. (A) situation   (B) situate
   (C) to situate   (D) situated

3. (A) make   (B) to be made
   (C) is made   (D) making

4. (A) end   (B) will be ended
   (C) to be ended   (D) has ended

Questions 5-9 refer to the following e-mail exchange.

To: blanc@fsu.net
From: sgentry@yahoo.com
Subject: French Class

Hello Professor Blanc,

My name is Shannon Gentry, and I'm in your French 104 class every Tuesday and Thursday from 1:00 to 3:20. I really enjoy the class, get along with my classmates, and think you are a good professor, but I'm really struggling in class. I studied French in high school and found it much easier. I study hard every day, do my homework, and try to speak in class, but I'm still having a tough time. I'm getting very discouraged. Do you have any advice?

Sincerely,

Shannon Gentry

To: sgentry@yahoo.com
From: blanc@fsu.net

Hi, Shannon,

Thanks for writing. Don't be discouraged. It takes a long time to learn a language. I think you're a good student, and you are doing the right things. Here are some more ideas to help you improve your French.

Watch movies and TV shows in French. Don't try to understand every word. Just enjoy the shows.
Listen to songs in French.
Read books in French. Don't look up every word you don't understand in the dictionary. It's better to try to guess the meaning from the story.
Try to find someone you can exchange e-mails with in French.

If you have any other questions, don't hesitate to ask.

Professor Blanc

---

5. What does Shannon think of her French class?
   (A) She thinks it's boring.   (B) She wants to stop attending it.
   (C) She really hates it.   (D) She really enjoys it.

6. What does Shannon NOT do to improve her French?
   (A) Study hard every day   (B) Do her homework
   (C) Watch movies in French   (D) Try to speak French in class

7. What did Shannon think of high school French.
   (A) She found it much easier.
   (B) She found it much more difficult.
   (C) She found it discouraging.
   (D) She didn't study French in high school.

8. Which one is NOT one of Professor Blanc's suggestions?
   (A) To listen to songs in French
   (B) To read books in French
   (C) To visit France
   (D) To watch movies in French

9. What does Professor Blanc say about learning a new language?
   (A) It is very difficult.
   (B) It takes a long time to learn a new one.
   (C) It its easy to learn a new one.
   (D) Studying a new language is a waste of time.

Self Review

☑ 전치사에 대해 아는 대로 써보세요. 그리고 다시 한번 복습하시기 바랍니다!!!

형태와 역할	
시점과 기간의 전치사	
시간의 전치사	
장소의 전치사	
주요 전치사	

MEMO

13 chapter

CONJUNCTION

Chapter 13 CONJUNCTION

Unit 01 접속사의 개념

1. 단어, 구, 절, 문장에 대한 이해

① 단어

② 구

③ 절

④ 문장

2. 명사절/ 형용사절/ 부사절 개념

① 명사절

② 형용사절

③ 부사절

Unit 02 접속사의 종류

1. 등위접속사

① 등위접속사의 종류

and, but(=yet), or

② 등위접속사의 특성

ⓐ 앞뒤로 동일구조를 가짐(병렬/등위 구조). 그리고 동일요소는 생략 가능

종류	예문
명사–명사	Tom and Jane had lunch together yesterday. Would you like soup or salad?
동사–동사	From man defeated Mandarin and then rescued.
형용사–형용사	I am an intelligent but modest person. This movie is both interesting and instructive.
부사–부사	He solved the problem easily and quickly. The mission must be finished neither late nor imperfectly.
부정사–부정사	I help my mother either to clean or (to) do the dishes every day. She likes to play tennis and (to) go shopping.

동명사-동명사	I enjoy playing computer games and watching TV. Jane likes not only listening to music but also play the piano.
전/명/구-전/명/구	Put the book on the table or under the table. The office is not near the station but farther down the alley.

CheckUp 1. Select the best answer to complete each sentence.

1. Come (and, but) see these movies on the big screen.

2. You will need dedication and (patient, patience) to survive there.

      ⓑ S+V, so/for S+V구조는 생략 불가

      ⓒ and, but(=yet), or, so, for 문두에 올 수 없다.

      ⓓ 3개 이상 나열 시: 명사, 명사, and 명사

  ③ A and B + 복수동사

     A but B + B에 일치하는 동사 (근접원리법)

     A or B + B에 일치하는 동사 (근접원리법)

2. 상관접속사의 의미와 수일치

① He and his father live in Daegu.

  Both she and her daughter live in Seoul.

  cf. *Romeo and Juliet* was written by Shakespeare.

② Either you or your sister has to pick him up at the airport.

③ Neither you nor I am responsible for it.

④ Not only he but also you were invited to the party.

  (= You as well as he were invited to the party.)

CheckUp 2. Select the best answer to complete each sentence.

1. The new policy applies to both full-timers (and, but) part-timers.

2. Neither the employers (nor, or) the employees will be satisfied with the new company policy.

3. Not Mr. Ames but you (is, are) the person to take care of the problem.

Unit 03 명사절 접속사

1. 명사절은 문장에서 주어, 목적어, 보어로 사용되는 것

① 주어

② 타동사의 목적어

③ 전치사의 목적어

④ 보어

2. that vs. what

① 둘 다 "~하는 것"으로 해석

② 주어, 목적어, 보어 자리에 다 올 수 있음

③ 뒷문장이 완전하면 that이 정답이지만, 뒷문장이 불완전하면 what이 정답

3. if vs. whether

① 둘 다 "인지 ~ 아닌지"로 해석

② if 뒤에는 반드시 주어+동사, whether는 변형 가능

③ if절은 타동사 뒤만 사용, whether는 4가지 패턴 모두 사용

	if	whether
명사절	– "~인지 ~아닌지" – 타동사 뒤에만 위치	– "~인지 ~아닌지" – 주어, 목적어, 보어 자리에 위치
부사절	– "만약 ~라면" – 주로 조건문, 가정문에 사용 – If+S+V~, S+V+O/C	– "~이든 ~아니든" – S+V+O/C (whether+ S+V+O/C)

4. 명사절 접속사 (~인지 아닌지)

① if, whether(명사절)의 차이점

whether s+v or not, whether or not s+v, whether (or not) to원형 (or not), whether A or B (상관접속사) – 다양한 변형 가능

if s+v (or not)는 이러한 형태 밖에 사용하지 못함(즉, 타동사 뒤 목적절만 가능)

② 부사절 접속사

if s+v:~라면

whether s+v:~이든 아니든

5. 의문사절=명사절 접속사

cf. 관계대명사와 관계부사와의 구별 필요

① 의문사의 종류(의문대명사, 의문형용사, 의문부사)
  ⓐ 의문대명사
     who, whom, what, which
  ⓑ 의문형용사
     whose, what, which
  ⓒ 의문부사
     when, where, why, how
② 의문사의 쓰임
  ⓐ 의문사 +(주어) + 동사
     I wonder where you were born.
     I don't know what you have.
  ⓑ 의문사 to부정사
     I want to know what I should do.
     = I want to know what to do.

Unit 04 복합 관계대명사

1. 복합 관계대명사의 종류

	명사절	부사절
whoever	anyone who ~하는 누구든지	no matter who 누가 ~할지라도
whosever	anyone whose 누구의 ~든지	no matter whose 누구의 ~를 할지라도
whomever	anyone whom ~하는 누구든지	no matter whom 누구를 ~할지라도
whichever	anything that ~하는 어떤 것이든지	no matter which 어떤 것을 ~할지라도
whatever	anything that ~하는 무엇이든지	no matter what 무엇을 ~할지라도

① 명사절 접속사
   Whoever wishes to succeed must work hard.
   Give the key to whomever you meet in the office.
   You can choose whatever you like.
   You may take whichever you like.
② 부사절 접속사(주로 양보의 의미)
   Whoever may say so, I will not believe it.
   Whatever he may do, he will not succeed in life.

2. 복합 관계형용사

whatever + 명사 무슨 ~이든지 (= no matter what +명사)	
whichever + 명사 무슨 ~이든지 (= no matter which + 명사)	

They can check the data bank for whatever software they need.

Whichever team has the highest production quota will be rewarded.

3. 복합 관계부사

Whenever 언제든지 (=no matter when, every time)	
Wherever 어디에서든지 (=no matter where)	
However 아무리 ~할지라도 (=no matter how)	

Come to me whenever you want.

Notebook makes it possible to work wherever you are.

However tired you may be, you have to finish the work.

Unit 05 부사절 접속사

구분	접속사+주어+동사	전치사+명사
양보	although, though, even if, even though	despite, in spite of, with all, for all
이유	because, since, as, now that, seeing that, for	because of, due to, owing to, on account of, in view of
시간	when, while, as, as soon as before/after, until, the moment, at the time SV, SV	during
조건	if, in case, once, as long as=as far as, provided(=providing), unless, suppose=supposing, on condition that,	in case of
목적	so that~can/may=in order that	so as to, in order to, to do
~함에 따라	according as	according to
~인 것처럼	as if, as though	like
매우 ~해서 ~하다	so~that, such~that	
복합관계사	따로 설명	

Practice Test A

✅ 다음 빈칸에 가장 적절한 것을 고르시오.

1) Your package sounds very attractive, _____ I'm afraid I can't accept it right now.
(A) and   (B) so   (C) but   (D) both

2) Not only the team members _____ also the supervisor suggested promoting Jack.
(A) and   (B) or   (C) nor   (D) but

3) Neither Jane nor Alice _____ the concert at the moment.
(A) enjoy   (B) enjoys   (C) is enjoying   (D) are enjoying

4) It is a well-known fact _____ regular exercise and a healthy diet reduce the risk of heart attacks.
(A) that   (B) whom   (C) who   (D) which

5) I have been a member of the committee _____ it was first established.
(A) as   (B) once   (C) when   (D) since

6) It is the same material, _____ the texture seems totally different.
(A) because   (B) if
(C) notwithstanding that   (D) so

7) _____ there was a budget cut, the project was successful.
(A) Although   (B) In spite of   (C) Because of   (D) Due to

8) He was feeling bad. _____, he tried to finish his speech.
(A) As a result   (B) Therefore   (C) However   (D) For example

9) The Daily Week mentioned _____ Great Insurance has a plan to acquire Sure Insurance.
(A) that   (B) which   (C) what   (D) who

10) _____ you are admitted to college or not will be announced on April 19 at the latest.
(A) that   (B) whether   (C) what   (D) which

Practice Test B

1) I turned on the air conditioner _____ the room was too hot.
(A) although   (B) however   (C) due to   (D) because

2) I am looking for a job in _____ web design or internet commerce.
(A) neither   (B) nor   (C) either   (D) other

3) The event is _____ popular that there will be a large crowd at the stadium.
(A) very   (B) too   (C) more   (D) so

4) Employees should contact Thomson _____ there are mistakes in their wages.
(A) prevented form   (B) only if
(C) asking for   (D) all about

5) He could not go out with her until _____.
(A) they allowed to do so   (B) she allowed to do so
(C) he allowed to do so   (D) allowed to do so

6) Neon is said to be inert _____ does not react easily with other substances.
(A) because of it   (B) because it
(C) it is because   (D) is because it

7) _____, their nests well, but also build them well.
(A) Not only brown thrashers protect
(B) Protect no only brown thrashers
(C) Brown thrashers not only protect
(D) Not only protect brown thrashers

8) A legislative body has the power not only to pass new laws, _____ repeal laws that have been passed earlier.
(A) to   (B) but also to   (C) and to   (D) in order to

9) He walked warily _____ he should fall.
(A) lest   (B) unless   (C) except   (D) before

10) The ship changed its course _____ there was a storm.
(A) on account of   (B) due to
(C) because of   (D) because

Practice Test C

☑ 밑줄 친 부분 중 어법상 어색한 곳을 고르시오.

1) Meerschaum is so <u>light</u> that <u>will it</u> <u>float</u> <u>in water</u>.
　　　　　　　　　　　A　　　　　B　　C　　　D

2) <u>Author</u> Sarah Orne Jewett <u>published her</u> first story <u>when was</u> nineteen <u>years</u>
　　A　　　　　　　　　　　　　　　B　　　　　　　　　　C　　　　　　　D
old.

3) The <u>architect</u> <u>must be</u> <u>both</u> a scientist and <u>artistic</u>.
　　　　A　　　　　B　　　C　　　　　　　　　　D

4) Rubber can be <u>made</u> <u>too</u> elastic that it <u>will stretch</u> more than nine times <u>its</u>
　　　　　　　　A　　B　　　　　　　　　　C　　　　　　　　　　　　D
normal length.

5) <u>Generally</u> alcohols <u>are</u> neutral compounds <u>displaying</u> neither acid <u>or</u> alkaline.
　　A　　　　　　　　　B　　　　　　　　　　　　C　　　　　　　　　D

6) The element ruthenium is <u>hard</u> and brittle, and <u>does</u> not dissolve <u>in</u> either
　　　　　　　　　　　　　　A　　　　　　　　　　B　　　　　　　　C
water <u>nor</u> acid.
　　　　D

7) <u>An American</u> is <u>not merely</u> confident but <u>is ambitious</u> and <u>loves</u> freedom.
　　A　　　　　　　B　　　　　　　　　　　C　　　　　　　D

8) <u>The onion</u> <u>has</u> both a <u>distinctive</u> flavor <u>or</u> odor.
　　A　　　　B　　　　　C　　　　　　D

9) From <u>its</u> beginning in 1639, Newport was <u>a</u> haven for colonial privateers <u>as</u>
　　　　A　　　　　　　　　　　　　　　　　　B　　　　　　　　　　　　　　C
<u>well</u> a major port for <u>trade</u>.
　　　　　　　　　　D

10) My nose as well as my ears <u>were</u> bleeding <u>when</u> the doctor <u>was</u> <u>brought in</u>.
　　　　　　　　　　　　　　　　A　　　　　　B　　　　　　　　　C　　D

Reading Comprehension

Questions 1-4 refer to the following article.

Many of the products that people in the Northern hemisphere depend on 1._____ in the warmer climates of the tropics. The prices consumers pay for these commodities 2._____ in real terms over the last 40 years, but the cost of fertilizers, pesticides, machinery and equipment has increased substantially. As a result of this, many of the people who 3._____ these crops have to work harder and longer for less money. Several years ago, a foundation 4._____ up to buy products at a fair price from farmers' organizations to prevent this from continuing to happen.

1. (A) produce   (B) had been produced
    (C) are produced   (D) have produced

2. (A) have not raised   (B) have not risen
    (C) do not raise   (D) do not rise

3. (A) would grow   (B) will have grown
    ((C) are being grown   (D) grow

4. (A) was set   (B) set
    (C) has been set   (D) sets

Questions 5-7 refer to the following memo.

To: Charles Dalloway
From: Clarissa Wolf
Date: August 18, 2006
Subject: Alternative Methods of Payment for Overseas Customers

There are now a number of alternative payment methods available to us.

Check. This is alow and will include bank charges.
Bank Draft. This is much quicker, but also includes charges.
Electronic Transfer. This is the quickest method, but the bank charges are the highest.

Please let me know your preference, and I will communicate it to our suppliers.

5. Why is this memo written?
   (A) To give information about payment methods
   (B) To ask Dalloway to pay fast
   (C) To ask for information about payment methods
   (D) To request the delay of the payment

6. Who is the memo sent to?
   (A) Bank tellers   (B) Charles Dalloway
   (C) Clarissa Wolf   (D) Overseas customers

7. Which method is the most expensive?
   (A) Bank draft   (B) Check
   (C) Electronic transfer   (D) Cash

Self Review

☑ 접속사에 대해 아는 대로 써보세요. 그리고 다시 한번 복습하시기 바랍니다!!!

접속사의 종류	
등위접속사	
종속접속사	
명사절 종속접속사	
부사절 종속접속사	

MEMO

RELATIVES

Practice Test
Reading Comprehension
Self Review

Chapter 14 RELATIVES

Unit 01 관계사절 (=형용사절 접속사)

관계대명사는 접속사 역할(관계)과 앞의 명사(대명사) 두 가지 역할을 동시에 한다. 따라서, 관계대명사 앞에는 선행사가 있어야 하며, 절이므로 문장과 문장을 이어주어야 한다.

	주격	소유격	목적격	
사람	who	whose	whom	형용사절
사물	which	whose /of which	which	
사람, 사물	that	x	that	
선행사가 없는 경우	what	x	what	명사절

1. 관계사가 맞는지 확인하는 방법

① 선행사가 사람인지 사물인지 확인
② 관계사절 내에서 관계대명사의 격을 확인
   + 동사면 주격을
   + 주어 + 타동사면 목적격을
   + 주어 + 자동사 + 전치사 + 이면 목적격을
   + 명사면 소유격을 사용

2. 선행사가 없는 경우는 what이 정답

3. 빈칸 앞에 comma가 있으면, 대개는 which가 정답(앞에 있는 단어 및 문장 전체 수식)

CheckUp 1. Select the best answer to complete each sentence.

1. The client (which, who) visited us yesterday called this morning.
2. The post office (which, who) is near the office is closed now.
3. She interviewed the director (who, whose) film won an award.
4. He is reading a long book, the author (of which, that) is also his professor.

Unit 02 관계대명사 that, what

1. 관계대명사 that, what

that	주격	This is a lady that wants to see you. I like the man that plays the piano now.
	목적격	This is the most useful book that I have ever read. That is the very car that I wanted to buy.
what	주어	What he said proved to be true. What I ordered hasn't arrived yet.
	보어	That what I'm saying.
	목적어	I like what she bought for my birthday. There is some truth in what he said.

① comma나 전치사가 있으면, 그 뒤에는 that은 절대 안 됨
② 선행사가 사람+사물이 동시에 있을 때(하나만 있어도 자유롭게 사용 가능)
③ the 최상급, the only, the same, every, all 등이 선행사 앞에 있으면 that

CheckUp 2. Select the best answer to complete each sentence.
1. Our new CEO, (that, who) started last week, is highly respected.
2. There will be a minimum investment of $10 million in Tech, Inc., (that, which) will help the company develop new products.

2. that vs. what

that	what
선행사 + that	what(선행사 포함)
형용사절 역할	명사절 역할
that + 불완전한 문장	what + 불완전한 문장

CheckUp 3. Select the best answer to complete each sentence.
1. The editor is reviewing the article (what, that) he wrote yesterday.
2. Her prompt reply is (what, which) impressed me the most.
3. The main purpose of this study is to share (that, what) we learned from this experience.

Unit 03 관계대명사절 문장 구조

1. 관계사속 동사는 정동사

    ① 단/복수 일치

    ② 능동/수동태 구조

2. 관계사절은 불완전한 문장이고 중복 불가

3. 관계사의 생략

    ① "관계대명사 주격+be동사" 생략가능

    ② 관계사 목적격 생략

Unit 04 관계부사

1. 관계부사의 종류

시간 – the time	when	– '접속사+부사'의 개념 – 선행사는 생략가능 – 관계부사 뒤에는 완전한 문장이 따라옴 – 관계부사 = 전치사 + 관계대명사 – the way 와 how는 동시에 사용하지 않음
장소 – the place	where	
이유 – the reason	why	
방법 – the way	how	

2. 관계부사와 관계대명사의 차이점

Unit 05 복합 관계부사

1. 관계사 vs. 복합 관계사의 차이점

2. 복합 관계대명사 vs. 복합 관계부사의 차이점

3. 각 복합관계사의 쓰임새 정리

CheckUp 4. Select the best answer to complete each sentence.

1. Those who (take, takes) physical exercise live longer.

2. (Who, Whoever) buys this house is very lucky.

3. Take (that, whatever) you want.

4. The city (which, where) we spent our summer vacation was beautiful.

5. Monday is the day (which, when) comes after Sunday.

6. Could you tell me the reason (which, why) you don't like me?

7. This is (the way, the way how) I solved the math question.

8. (Whenever, Wherever) you go, you will find Coca-Cola.

9. I stay with Jane anytime (when, whenever) I go to L.A.

10. People always want more, (how, however) rich they are.

Practice Test A

☑ 다음 빈칸에 가장 적절한 것을 고르시오.

1) George is the _____ sent the mail.
(A) he who has   (B) those who have
(C) one who has   (D) ones who have

2) Those are the people _____ I gave the information.
(A) to who   (B) to whom   (C) to which   (D) to that

3) _____ laugh last laugh longest.
(A) He who   (B) He whom   (C) Those who   (D) Those whom

4) Linda is the student _____ I think is the best in the school.
(A) who   (B) whom   (C) whose   (D) which

5) It is the first step _____ the most difficult.
(A) who is   (B) which are   (C) that is   (D) that are

6) I want to give you _____ you need.
(A) that   (B) what
(C) the thing what   (D) ∅

7) They always give the best seat to _____ comes first.
(A) which   (B) whom   (C) whomever   (D) whoever

8) I have three best friends, one of _____ is a famous film director.
(A) who   (B) whom   (C) that   (D) them

9) The Good Earth, _____, is a novel about China.
(A) was written by Pearl Buck
(B) which written by Pearl Buck
(C) which was written by Pearl Buck
(D) that was written by Pearl Buck

10) The tree, _____ are almost bare now, is more than three hundred years old.
(A) the whose branches   (B) the branches of which
(C) of which branches   (D) the branches of whose

Practice Test B

1) A vacation is a period of the year _____ schools are officially closed.
(A) which   (B) where   (C) when   (D) why

2) Summer is the season _____ is between spring and autumn.
(A) which   (B) in which   (C) when   (D) in that

3) Greece is the country _____ the Olympics started.
(A) which   (B) where   (C) when   (D) why

4) A cafe is a small restaurant _____ people can get a light meal.
(A) which   (B) where   (C) at which   (D) at where

5) The reason _____ she didn't hear the phone is that she is a bit deaf.
(A) which   (B) for which   (C) why   (D) for why

6) Adding −ed is _____ you form the regular past tense in English.
(A) the way   (B) how   (C) the way how   (D) in how

7) Do you recommend _____ you stayed during summer vacation?
(A) the hotel   (B) where
(C) the hotel which   (D) the hotel where

8) Call me _____ you need my help.
(A) anytime which   (B) whenever
(C) no matter when   (D) no matter whenever

9) You will find good people _____ you go.
(A) any place which   (B) any place where
(C) any place wherever   (D) wherever

10) _____ he eats, he never gets fat.
(A) How much   (B) Matter much
(C) No matter much   (D) No matter how much

Practice Test C

✅ 밑줄 친 부분 중 어법상 어색한 곳을 고르시오.

1) The doctor, <u>who office</u> was newly <u>decorated</u>, started <u>to charge</u> higher <u>fees</u>.
            A   B   C   D

2) <u>Engineering</u> is a profession <u>who</u> puts <u>scientific</u> knowledge <u>to</u> practical use.
   A   B   C   D

3) <u>All the</u> people <u>who is</u> interested <u>in Biology</u> should <u>be invited to</u> the lecture.
   A   B   C   D

4) The telephone number, <u>that</u> is <u>written</u> down <u>on the envelope</u>, is <u>for the</u>
                          A   B   C
   hotel.
   D

5) The chairs <u>which were</u> <u>in bad condition</u> <u>was sent</u> out to <u>be repaired</u>.
                A   B   C   D

6) The president, <u>supporting</u> by <u>all the people</u>, felt <u>confident</u> <u>about the future</u>.
                A   B   C   D

7) You <u>can choose</u> the thing <u>what</u> you want <u>to have</u> for your birthday present
         A   B   C
   in this <u>toy</u> store.
         D

8) You can invite <u>anyone whoever</u> <u>wants</u> <u>to come</u> <u>to your</u> birthday party.
                A   B   C   D

9) Paris, <u>the capital</u> of France, <u>it is</u> one of the most beautiful <u>cities</u> <u>in the</u>
          A   B   C
   world.
   D

10) <u>It is</u> the meteorologists that <u>is trying</u> <u>to analyze</u> and forecast <u>the weather</u>.
   A   B   C   D

Questions 1-4 refer to the following news report.

In 1830, the population of the world 1._____ about one billion. In 1975, there were almost four billion people in the world. If this population growth 2._____, there will be seven billion people by the end of 2020. The present food supply is being increased by cultivating more land. However, the population 3._____ faster than the food supply. Already, about 500 million people barely get enough to eat, and about three million people die of malnutrition every year. Overpopulation also 4._____ pollution and reduces the quality of life.

1. (A) is   (B) was
   (C) were   (D) has been

2. (A) has continued   (B) will have continued
   (C) continued   (D) continues

3. (A) is increasing   (B) increase
   (C) to increase   (D) will have increase

4. (A) to cause   (B) causing
   (C) causes   (D) is caused

Questions 5-7 refer to the following memo.

FAX COVER SHEET

Attention: David Montgomery

From: Colin Scott

No. of pages: 2

Please telephone us immediately if you do not receive the number of pages indicated.

Re: Lunch Arrangements

Dear David,

With reference to our phone conversation yesterday, I am writing to confirm that we can provide lunch for 9 people in your executive suite at 1 p.m. on Friday, the 24th of February. On the next page are two alternative menus. I would be grateful if you could let me know which one you would prefer by February 16th.

If you have any further questions, please do not hesitate to ask.

Sincerely,

Colin Scott

Colin Scott

---

5. What information does Mr. Scoot wish to receive?
   (A) Confirmation of the arrangements
   (B) Details of the lunch prices
   (C) More information about the location
   (D) A decision on what option is wanted

6. When does Mr. Scott need information by?
   (A) As soon as possible   (B) February 16th
   (C) February 24th   (D) This weekend

7. Who sent this fax?
   (A) Colin Scott   (B) David Montgomery
   (C) Executives   (D) Not given

Questions 8-12 refer to the following advertisement and notice.

SUMMER VACATION SPECIAL!

Joanne's Beautiful Crafts is offering a summer vacation special on its craft workshops. During the months of June, July, and August, Joanne's Beautiful Crafts will offer a 2-for-1 special. Take any one of our craft workshops, and we will enroll you in another workshop of your choice free of charge.

We offer a variety of classes in scrapbooking, floral design, painting interior decorating. framing. calligraphy, and more. We offer group classes as well as private lessons with a certified instructor in each area.

Which classes are offered varies by week and month with schedules posted on our website. Classes fill up quickly, so hurry to register!

Attention Staff:

We should be getting many new participants in our summer workshops with the advertising of our 2-for-1 special. If you are available and have skill in any of the workshop areas. we will need staff to work extra hours.

If you would like to volunteer to work more hours or know someone with skills in these areas, please sign up on the list below or notify me by e-mail. Also, specify which additional days you are able to work. However, nobody may work more thank 40 hours a week.

Thank you for your cooperation.

Monica Salvatore

---

8. What is the summer special?

   (A) Free classes

   (B) Pay for one class, and get the second class free

   (C) No registration fee

   (D) No registration fee, two classes free

9. What does Ms. Salvatore ask the staff for if they sign up?

   (A) Dates available   (B) Work phone number

   (C) To work more than a week (D) Group classes

10. In which of the following months does the summer special NOT apply?

    (A) May   (B) June

    (C) July   (D) August

11. What is the purpose of the notice?

    (A) To inform the staff of the new policy

    (B) To ask for volunteers to work extra hours

    (C) To inform the staff of the summer special

    (D) To ask for volunteers to be instructors

12. How many classes are offered for the summer special?

    (A) Seven   (B) Nine

    (C) Ten   (D) It does not say.

Self Review

☑ 관계사에 대해 아는 대로 써보세요. 그리고 다시 한번 복습하시기 바랍니다!!!

역할	
that, what	
관계사 문장 구조	
관계부사	
복합관계부사	

Fresh TOEIC_Answer

Chapter 01 Verb

Checkup 1 1. rises 2. raise 3. sits 4. lies
Checkup 2 1. is 2. remain
Checkup 3 1. is 2. calm 3. false 4. sad 5. soft
Checkup 4 1. me the bill 2. for his children 3. it to me

Practice Test A

1) B 2) B 3) C 4) A/D 5) D 6) B 7) B 8) A 9) B 10) C

Practice Test B

1) D 2) D 3) C 4) C 5) A 6) D 7) D 8) C 9) B 10) C

Practice Test C

1) A(had)   2) D(sweet)   3) B(kill)
4) B(it out)   5) D(get along with him) 6) C(makes)
7) A(take)   8) D(rises)   9) C(is getting)
10) B(happen)

Reading Comprehension

1. D 2. C 3. A 4. B 5. A 6. C 7. C

Chapter 02 Tense

Checkup 1 1. boils 2. is boiling 3. snows 4. provides 5. encourages
Checkup 2 1. will rain 2. will understand 3. see 4. is 5. will come
Checkup 3 1. will live 2. are going to 3. will 4. will hire 5. will get
Checkup 4 1. visited 2. lived 3. worked 4. said
Checkup 5 1. has commuted 2. have been waiting 3. will have been teaching
           4. has visited 5. has lived
Checkup 6 1. had entered 2. had been 3. broke
Checkup 7 1. will have taught 2. will have finished
Checkup 8 1. has moved 2. received
Checkup 9 1. was watching 2. was gradually losing
Checkup 10 1. likes 2. remains

Practice Test A

1) A   2) C   3) A   4) B   5) B   6) C   7) C   8) D   9) D   10) D

Practice Test B

1) B   2) B   3) A   4) D   5) A   6) D   7) D   8) C   9) B   10) A

Practice Test C

1) C(was)   2) C(will go/am going)   3) C(was launched)
4) C(will be practicing)   5) B(began)   6) C(has studied)
7) A(have had)   8) C(has grown)   9) D(are hatched)
10) C(had written)

Reading Comprehension

1. A   2. D   3. C   4. B   5. D   6. A   7. B

Chapter 03 Noun

Checkup 1 1. contamination   2. Joblessness
Checkup 2 1. plane ticket   2. flower
Checkup 3 1. assistant   2. investors

Practice Test A

1) A   2) D   3) D   4) D   5) B   6) A   7) D   8) C   9) B   10) A

Practice Test B

1) C   2) B   3) D   4) C   5) A   6) D   7) B   8) B   9) B   10) A

Practice Test C

1) B(is)   2) B(is going to)   3) A(much)
4) B(needs)   5) B(two kinds)   6) A(only a little)
7) A(adheres)   8) B(possibility)   9) B(an)
10) C(Mount Everest)

Reading Comprehension

1. D   2. A   3. B   4. C   5. B   6. D   7. A

Chapter 04 Pronoun

Checkup 1 1. its 2. their 3. It is 4. They 5. him 6. his 7. yourself 8. themselves
Checkup 2 1. a friend of mine   2. a friend of my father's
Checkup 3 1. that   2. Those
Checkup 4 1. the other   2. another   3. the others   4. Another
Checkup 5 1. one another   2. each other

Checkup 6 1. the other 2. The others 3. others 4. other 5. another 6. another
          7. each other 8. every fourth yeaR
Checkup 7 1. Some 2. any

Practice Test A
1) A 2) B 3) C 4) B 5) D 6) A 7) C 8) C 9) B. C 10) D

Practice Test B
1) A 2) D 3) D 4) D 5) B 6) C 7) A 8) D 9) B 10) D

Practice Test C
1) C(he)   2) D(hers/her books)   3) D(their)
4) B(he or she)   5) C(Tom and me)   6) D(another)
7) C(the를 없앰)   8) C(himself or herself)   9) C(each other)
10) B(its)

Reading Comprehension
1. A 2. D 3. C 4. B 5. A 6. B 7. D

Chapter 05 Agreement

Checkup 1 1. attends 2. are 3. makes
Checkup 2 1. have 2. need
Checkup 3 1. support 2. has 3. work
Checkup 4 1. was 2. is 3. is 4. dies 5. have 6. envy 7. was 8. glitters 9. is 10. is
          11. are 12. are

Practice Test A
1) A 2) B 3) A 4) C 5) B 6) B 7) D 8) A 9) D 10) A

Practice Test B
1) C 2) B 3) D 4) C 5) A 6) B 7) C 8) A 9) A 10) B

Practice Test C
1) B(have)   2) B(is)   3) B(tries)
4) B(were)   5) B(plan)   6) A(are)
7) B(are)   8) D(has)   9) C(know)
10) B(instruct)

Reading Comprehension
1. C 2. B 3. A 4. D 5. B 6. A 7. D 8. C 9. A

Chapter 06 Adjective

Checkup 1 1. careful, carefully 2. well 3. good 4. terribly 5. hard, hardly 6. late, lately
7. completely forgot 8. have never 9. impossible 10. innovative

Checkup 2 1. a few 2. many

Practice Test A

1) B 2) A 3) B 4) A 5) B 6) D 7) D 8) C 9) B 10) B

Practice Test B

1) A 2) C 3) D 4) C 5) D 6) A 7) C 8) B 9) C 10) D

Practice Test C

1) B(special)   2) C(sweet)   3) D(damaged)
4) C(boring)   5) A(have)   6) A(interesting)
7) B(more correctly)   8) D(that of Korea) 9) B(think)
10) B(cities)

Reading Comprehension

1. A 2. B 3. D 4. C 5. D 6. C 7. B 8. A 9. B

Chapter 07 Adverb

Checkup 1 1. repeatedly 2. Finally
Checkup 2 1. still 2. already 3. very 4. usually

Practice Test A

1) A 2) C 3) B 4) D 5) B 6) B 7) A 8) A 9) B 10) C

Practice Test B

1) D 2) B 3) A 4) B 5) B 6) B 7) B 8) B 9) C 10) C

Practice Test C

1) A(Practically)   2) B(necessarily) 3) D(purely)
4) A(Recently)   5) D(somewhat)   6) B(regularly)
7) D(hard)   8) D(formally)   9) B(fast)
10) B(late)

Reading Comprehension

1. A 2. D 3. B 4. C 5. C 6. D 7. A

Chapter 08 Voice

Checkup 1 1. be sent 2. be awarded 3. was signed 4. been decorated 5. is considered
6. kept 7. are told

Checkup 2 1. was born 2. is located 3. by 4. for 5. to 6. with 7. by 8. of
9. from 10. to

Practice Test A
1) A   2) C   3) D   4) D   5) D   6) C   7) D   8) D   9) A   10) B

Practice Test B
1) C   2) B   3) D   4) B   5) A   6) B   7) C   8) C   9) C   10) A

Practice Test C
1) A(is ruled)   2) C(to be seen)   3) B(known for)
4) A(is said)   5) A(It is)   6) B(will be built)
7) D(make)   8) B(have been killed)   9) B(being elected)
10) D(can be reused)

Reading Comprehension
1. B   2. D   3. A   4. C   5. A   6. C   7. D

Chapter 09 Infinitive

Checkup 1 1. for a child 2. for a child 3. of her, ∅ 4. me 5. for you
Checkup 2 1. To make 2. to demonstrate
Checkup 3 1. to advertise 2. to hire
Checkup 4 1. to work 2. to enter
Checkup 5 1. to improve 2. to refuse
Checkup 6 1. to translate 2. translated 3. eat 4. finish 5. sing 6. cry
7. reserve 8. to redo
Checkup 7 1. To access 2. meet 3. to increase 4. to talk
Checkup 8 1. ∅ 2. me

Practice Test A
1) B   2) B   3) C   4) C   5) C   6) C   7) C   8) A   9) D   10) C

Practice Test B
1) C   2) A   3) D   4) A   5) D   6) A   7) D   8) B   9) B   10) C

Practice Test C
1) B(play/playing)   2) C(go)   3) B(repair)
4) B(of that man)   5) B(to be punished) 6) D(to live with)
7) B(it)   8) B(feel)   9) C(it)

10) C(to be seen)

Reading Comprehension
1. A   2. C   3. B   4. D   5. B   6. D   7. C

Chapter 10 Gerund

Checkup 1 1. being elected 2. not writing 3. is 4. are 5. being 6. travelling 7. taking
8. to repair 9. repairing 10. visiting

Practice Test A
1) C   2) C   3) D   4) D   5) C   6) D   7) B, C 8) A   9) B   10) C

Practice Test B
1) B   2) D   3) B   4) C   5) C   6) B   7) C   8) A   9) B   10) B

Practice Test C
1) A(Speaking/To speak)   2) C(is)   3) C(developing)
4) C(on)   5) B(interviewing) 6) D(being invited)
7) D(from developing)   8) A(The eating)   9) C(our)
10) A(to enclose)

Reading Comprehension
1. A   2. C   3. D   4. B   5. B   6. A   7. D

Chapter 11 Participle

Checkup 1 1. applying 2. confusing 3. reduced 4. suggested
Checkup 2 1. disappointing 2. pleased 3. satisfying
Checkup 3 1. barking 2. closed 3. developing 4. developed 5. surprised 6. surprising
7. good-looking 8. newly-built 9. man-made 10. eye-catching
Checkup 4 1. known 2. called 3. folded 4. working 5. named 6. pulled 7. buried
8. drowning 9. understood 10. invited
Checkup 5 1. Researching 2. Browsing
Checkup 6 1. was taken 2. had been 3. As 4. was 5. was 6. Considering 7. not
8. Having 9. Judging 10. Turning

Practice Test A
1) A   2) D   3) C   4) A   5) A   6) A   7) A   8) B   9) B   10) C

Practice Test B
1) C   2) D   3) D   4) B   5) C   6) D   7) B   8) B   9) B   10) C

Practice Test C

1) A(shocked)   2) C(convincing)   3) C(exciting)

4) A(frightening)   5) C(gathered)   6) D(written)

7) A(surrounded)   8) A(known)   9) B(interested)

10) A(lost)

Reading Comprehension

1. B   2. A   3. C   4. D   5. C   6. D   7. D   8. A   9. B

Chapter 12 Preposition

Checkup 1 1. leaving 2. us 3. by 4. throughout

Checkup 2 1. Due to 2. Thanks to

Checkup 3 1. on 2. in 3. along 4. out of

Checkup 4 1. except 2. notwithstanding 3. Considering 4. including

Checkup 5 1. in 2. into 3. at 4. over 5. next to 6. in 7. for 8. at 9. by 10. by

Practice Test A

1) B   2) A   3) C   4) C   5) C   6) A   7) A   8) C   9) B   10) B

Practice Test B

1) A   2) C   3) B   4) D   5) B   6) A   7) B   8) D   9) D   10) A

Practice Test C

1) B(in)   2) A(Like)   3) D(spreading)

4) B(the fact that she)   5) C(to fish)   6) D(easily)

7) C(cleaned the house)   8) C(walking)   9) C(however, nevertheless)

10) B(is)

Reading Comprehension

1. A   2. D   3. C   4. B   5. D   6. C   7. A   8. C   9. B

Chapter 13 Conjunction

Checkup 1 1. and 2. patience

Checkup 2 1. and 2. nor 3. are

Practice Test A

1) C   2) D   3) C   4) A   5) D   6) C   7) A   8) C   9) A   10) B

Practice Test B

1) D   2) C   3) D   4) B   5) D   6) B   7) A   8) B   9) A   10) D

Practice Test C

1) B(it will)   2) C(when she was)   3) D(an artist)

4) B(so)
5) D(nor)
6) D(or)

7) C(ambitious)
8) D(and)
9) C(as well as)

10) A(was)

Reading Comprehension
1. C   2. B   3. D   4. A   5. A   6. B   7. C

Chapter 14 Relatives

Checkup 1   1. who   2. which   3. whose   4. of which
Checkup 2   1. who   2. which
Checkup 3   1. that   2. what   3. what
Checkup 4   1. take   2. Whoever   3. whatever   4. where   5. which   6. why   7. the way
                8. Wherever   9. when   10. however

Practice Test A
1) C   2) B   3) C   4) A   5) C   6) B   7) D   8) B   9) C   10) B

Practice Test B
1) C   2) A   3) B   4) B/C   5) B/C   6) A/B   7) D   8) B   9) D   10) D

Practice Test C
1) A(whose office)
2) B(which/that)
3) B(who are)

4) A(which)
5) C(were sent)
6) A(supported)

7) B(that)
8) A(anyone who/ whoever)
9) B(is)

10) B(are)

Reading Comprehension
1. B   2. A   3. D   4. C   5. D   6. B   7. A   8. B   9. A   10. A   11. B   12. D

이정복

계명대학교 Tabula Rasa College 교수

저서
TOEFL PRIMER
절친 영문법
대학기초영어
기초영어의 활용

Fresh TOEIC

초판발행	2021년 3월 15일
지은이	이정복
펴낸이	안종만 · 안상준
편 집	정수정
기획/마케팅	장규식
표지디자인	BEN STORY
제 작	고철민 · 조영환
펴낸곳	(주)**박영사**
	서울특별시 금천구 가산디지털2로 53, 210호(가산동, 한라시그마밸리)
	등록 1959. 3. 11. 제300-1959-1호(倫)
전 화	02)733-6771
f a x	02)736-4818
e-mail	pys@pybook.co.kr
homepage	www.pybook.co.kr
ISBN	979-11-303-1261-3 93740

* 파본은 구입하신 곳에서 교환해 드립니다. 본서의 무단복제행위를 금합니다.
* 저자와 협의하여 인지첨부를 생략합니다.

정 가   15,000원